THREE GREAT IRISHMEN
Shaw, Yeats, Joyce

ARLAND USSHER
("Portrait of a Young Man")
By Augustus John

THREE GREAT IRISHMEN

Shaw, Yeats, Joyce

by

ARLAND USSHER

With Portraits by
AUGUSTUS JOHN

NEW YORK
THE DEVIN-ADAIR COMPANY
1953

TO

MY FATHER

*Printed in Great Britain
by the Camelot Press Ltd.,
London and Southampton*

CONTENTS

ACKNOWLEDGMENTS

My thanks are due to Mrs. W. B. Yeats for permission to quote from her husband's work, and also for reading through the proofs of my second chapter.

My thanks are due to the Fitzwilliam Museum, Cambridge, to the National Gallery of Sweden, to Col. Eric Phillips, Toronto, and to Mr. George Joyce for permission to reproduce portraits in their possession; to the Irish Department of External Affairs for their helpfulness in enabling me to procure reproductions; and above all to Mr. Augustus John, O.M., R.A., for granting me permission to use his works in the first place, and for his consistent generous co-operation.

A.U.

ILLUSTRATIONS

PREFACE

THIS BOOK IS AN extension of an essay of mine
The Magi, published in *The Dublin Magazine* (Spring
number 1945). In it I attempt to assess three figures
with whom, by the accident of my birth and upbringing,
I feel a certain affinity, and whose influence on me—
partly for that reason—has been strong. They are also
of course powerful influences on the whole of 20th
Century literature and thought—even when they are
unconscious ones. But I believe that without some knowledge of their Irish background, none of them—not even
Shaw—can really be understood; and James Joyce
presents the paradox of an experimenter in form whose
material is as local and ancestral as Glasnevin Cemetery.
Thirty years ago, to praise James Joyce was an act of
some daring; today it needs an almost equal daring to
criticise him. For my part, I seem compelled to commit
both of these solecisms; I was always an enthusiast in
regard to *Ulysses*—I am not yet converted to *Finnegans
Wake*, though I keep returning to that work (as I first
read the "trailers" in *transition*) with the assiduity of a
mouse nibbling at a hard and unbroken loaf. But I do
not believe one can fully comprehend either Joyce's
achievement or his limitations without having some
acquaintance with the Irish character, and even with
that character as reflected in Gaelic literature—a
literature of which Joyce was, of course, almost wholly
ignorant. It is more important to the student even than
a knowledge—doubtless extremely helpful—of the
geography of Dublin. James Joyce is the first Irishman
of genius (as distinct from the descendants of the

9

Planters) who has attained to complete expression in English prose. Yeats, Anglo-Irishman as he knew himself to be, never really came out of his lonely Tower—that Tower from which (so to speak) the heroes of *Ulysses* set forth in the morning; and Shaw had little, except his strange spiritual isolation, that was properly Irish—he belonged to the old tradition of the London Irish comedy. But with Joyce—as Valéry Larbaud declared—Ireland re-enters (or rather first enters) world-literature; Anna Liffey—before him a "pale soft shy slim slip of a thing"—mingles crashingly with the salt ocean. For this reason among others, Joyce can be, to me, enormously exciting—more so even than W. B. Yeats, though that is saying much; and for the same reason he can appear uncouth and repellent. To contrast Shaw and Joyce, those two Aristophanean spirits, is to realise the growth of nationalism in the quarter-century that separates them—of nationalism in everything except what one may call the "technology" of the arts. Shaw was—almost—a cosmopolitan, whereas Joyce was an Irish literary technician who found it expedient to work abroad. In criticising James Joyce I am distressingly conscious of my audacity; not because I am impressed by the Joyce-cult of the moment—based on everything in his work which is least likely to be permanent—but because I have a very warm admiration for what seems to me his essential genius.

A word about the form of this book. I use here again the method which, in *The Face and Mind of Ireland*, I called "the continually shifting viewpoint". It is not merely that one likes and mislikes, but that one praises and censures for partly the same reasons. This "ambivalent" approach should need no apology in the age of psychoanalysis and relativity; and it would seem especially well adapted to the study of three characters who, whatever their divergences, were all of them masters of irony—even of "romantic" irony. Nevertheless it is an approach which is still apt to disconcert when employed in philosophy and literary criticism (and philosophy is properly criticism applied to existence itself as art-object). Few people can resign the notion that criticism should be pedagogic and that philosophy should be reformist; whereas a mind that can contemplate without prejudice should find the correctives and balances in the things themselves and their inter-relations. Thus I have chosen for my subjects the trio in question, not only because they are the three greatest Irishmen of this century, but also because they stand in a certain "dialectical" relation to each other. In an age when philosophy has forsaken the academical world for the world of the artist, they supply—by their complementary adequacies and inadequacies—something like a complete truth by which a man can live.

ARLAND USSHER.

GEORGE BERNARD SHAW

By Augustus John

I

Bernard Shaw:

EMPEROR AND CLOWN

I WRITE FRANKLY as one who was never a Shavian.
Even in ebullient boyhood Shaw scarcely evoked my
—generally lively—faculty for hero-worship. I had
other gods—W. B. Yeats, D. H. Lawrence, a few Ger-
mans, for a while the Chesterbelloc combination—but
never G. B. S. His mind lacked two things which I am still
romantic enough to prize—colour and mystery. Posterity
will perhaps call him the greatest man of our time, and
—I am afraid I would impatiently have said—I will not
dispute him with posterity. I have met not a few persons
—quiet natures, totally unknown to fame—with a far
greater subtlety of thought and range of perceptions
than ever Shaw had. That of course is not enough to
make them "great", but it shows the difficulty of the concept of greatness: a concept which G. B. S. himself—
schoolboyishly admiring "supermen"—was sometimes
much too free with. Swift and Voltaire had limitations
as great as his; but Swift and Voltaire had also the discretion not to set up as prophets. The thought of all
those committees, all those Fabian Summer Schools, was
too much for me; I felt about him as Marchbanks felt
about the prosaically-idealistic Morell—and was repelled
by something "phoney" in the Marchbanks side of his
character. And yet, if Shaw were buried in any Christian
grave—whether consecrate or not—I should hold the
spot in particular veneration. For there was nothing

common in him; and—what is, alas, rarer in a literary man—there was nothing mean.

This peculiar elevation of temper he always carried—like his fiercely, but gaily, tilted chin; his life was a disproof of the saying *Bel esprit mauvais caractère*. But I do not mean to imply, of course, that Shaw was—any more than Shelley was—altogether of angelic cast. The man who wrote *The Cenci* must have had some sinister possibilities, and the man who wrote *The Philanderer* (that comedy of vivisection, in all senses) had at least disquieting ones. "Good" artists, it is to be feared, cannot be quite good artists; and the dramatist, above all, must play out an inner drama. The point would hardly need stressing, were it not that Shaw was so often accorded an almost religious veneration—because, forsooth, he had no "vices"—a veneration which he seemed, indeed, at times to enjoy. It is ironical to remember that, after he wrote *Candida*, Shaw was hailed as a Defender of the Hearth, and that, after *Saint Joan*, he almost received popular canonisation as a Defender of the Faith—chiefly on account of the indifferent "poetic" passages in those plays. There is indeed a danger, unless some writer in the Latin lands produces a better Jeanne d'Arc (which scarcely at present exists) that Shaw's Joan may replace the historic one. G. K. Chesterton once said that G. B. S., in another age, would have been a great and devout saint; but I can imagine him more easily as Abélard than as St. Bernard. Chesterton's fancy was founded, of course, on the notion that Shaw was what is called a "puritan" —a suggestion that came rather ironically from the good G. K. Puritan—an idle, or rather an over-worked word: I know not what it means. If a puritan be someone who fears and suppresses the passions, on account of their strength, then Shaw was the least puritanic of men. It was indeed his chief limitation as philosopher and romancer that he had little conception—for good and ill—of what men have meant by Sin; in this sense he was not puritanical but essentially *pure*—though with a slightly "cellophane" sort of purity. His coldness was in fact that of the intellectualist rather than of the moralist; and he hardly knew the meaning of an "inhibition". Was Don Juan a puritan (or for that matter those other Shavian puppets—Charles II and Catharine of Russia)? Yet Shaw had much of Don Juan in him, and he himself was conscious of the affinity; he wrote one of his best scenes around it—in one of his most tedious plays. If he had, perhaps, few "affairs" it was because there were always so many women in his life, and more in his imagination,—he had not time to settle upon particular flowers. And he had, one suspects, something of that last perversity of the Don Juans—a coquettish or priggish pleasure in baffling the enamoured one, in refusing himself. The real Don Juan is cold because his sex is "in the head"; and cruelty is the dubious sort of sublimation effected by schoolboys, prisoners and dictators. It is the quality in Shaw that makes many of his leading puppets, whether male or female, to some tastes a trifle unpleasant —and it is the quality in him that made him understand modern women so well.

It would be as true (and, of course, as false) to call Shaw an epicure as a puritan; though he was an epicure, as Plato and Epicurus were, in thoughts more than in sensations. "I valued sexual experience" he said "because of its power of producing a celestial flood of emotion and exaltation which, however momentary, gave me a sample of the ecstasy that may one day be the normal condition of conscious intellectual activity." That is scarcely the remark of a puritan, but rather (to use his favourite term of abuse) of a very refined and introverted "voluptuary". Shaw enjoyed argument with an almost carnal passion; whereas your mere preacher hates argument, as your mere puritan fears flirtation. His aversion for animal food may have been partly due to the fact that vegetarian restaurants—in his youth and perhaps still—provided more interesting and diversified fare than the popular cook-shops. English cookery might well make vegetarians of us all. Besides this, of course, he was a kind-hearted man—except where his theories interfered. His humanitarianism reminds us perhaps—a little too much—of his friends, our ascetical dictators; and he resembled another British colonial, Kipling, in admiring toughness or Spartan rigour. In addition, I think he cultivated his eccentricity—as he cultivated his Irish voice—for the sake of doing an "act"; and it is interesting to speculate whether he would have persisted in his frugalities if prosperity had not come to him late, when his habits had hardened and the "Shaw legend" was already formed. He knew the public is more interested in an author's habits than in his ideas; and that if you talk for long enough about your habits, you may even find in the end that your ideas are being talked about. To be told what the great man eats gives almost the sensation which the French populace had, in being permitted to assist at the meals of the Grand Monarque.

However, when all deductions are made, it remains true that Shaw was slightly unbalanced on this subject of the Flesh—like so many of his countrymen. He was certainly on much worse terms with it than he was with the other two members of the famous trio; in fact he saw the Flesh—Manichean-wise—as the World and the Devil rolled in one. It was apparently impossible for him to imagine that a vegetarian frugal-living dictator could be worldly, and indeed devilish, in his aims. The fact is worth noting, because it led him into his worst and most dangerous lapses of judgment; and it is an impressive instance of the fruits of a false philosophy. The man who protested against Denshawai was unmoved by Dachau; and he failed entirely to note, in the experiments of the German camps, the natural conclusion of the materialist science which he so consistently attacked.

G. B. S.'s teetotalism is in a slightly different category; and it has been a little misconceived by writers who do not know the Irish atmosphere, and have in consequence written foolishly of Shaw's "narrow puritan home". In Ireland, drinking is not so much a weakness of the flesh as a form of flight from the flesh; and the pub is the layman's monastery. Shaw was not really a "good mixer", and I think he preferred "intelligent women" to intelligent men. Irish puritanism is a Catholic phenomenon even more than a Protestant one; but there is no equivalent in Ireland to the English "nonconformist conscience", touching such things as drink, cards or betting. If an Irishman eschews these diversions, it is not from a congenital moral tone, but usually from unhappy family experience—such as of course Shaw had had, in ample measure, with a tippling father. Anyhow, the thought that Shaw could ever have needed alcoholic stimulants would indeed be a good joke; one feels that a G. B. S. "under the influence" might have given vent to a merriment too loud for mortal ears, like one of the sons of God shouting for joy. I have seen Shaw sober, and any number of people drunk, and certainly Shaw was brighter than them all! The rattle of his stage-monologue can, indeed, become tedious, like the chatter of the alcoholic; but many of his playlets and fantasias exhibit the happy nonsensicality of a true son of Pantagruel. No doubt his indifference to the vine showed a certain gap in his culture: an inappreciation of the best part of tradition—of things slow-matured and "set", like orthography, church-ritual and menus. Culture to him was bourgeois; and he had perhaps a right to feel that way, because—a rare thing in a socialist—he was not by temperament a bourgeois. Even Lenin never called him that!

Which reminds one that Lenin said he was "a good man fallen among Fabians". The remark was probably less epigrammatic in the original Russian than in translation; for Lenin was not addicted to epigram. But it was in any case unapt; for Shaw created Fabianism more than Fabianism perverted Shaw. The excellent Mr. and Mrs. Webb, without him, would scarcely have carried it very far. One may wish, indeed, that Ireland—land of missionaries—had sent forth a Shaw to every European capital at the beginning of the century; the world today might wear a different aspect. But perhaps the collaboration, after all, was needed. "An English army led by an Irish general", said Shaw's Napoleon, might defeat a French army led by an Italian general. It is impossible not to suspect that Shaw was thinking of the Fabian campaigners—under his generalship: a combination which may—or may not—prove to have anticipated and disarmed the Marxian drive. As Wesley saved England from the French Revolution, so Shaw may have saved her from the Russian; the fact is of more importance than his uncritical admiration of the Soviets. Chesterton blamed Shaw for treading out "the last ember" of the French Revolution; but Chesterton was born too late to see the French Revolution—and he did not particularly like the Russian one when he saw it.

Fabian Socialism is essentially the English—I should say the Western or civilised—form of Socialism; and Shaw, more than any single man, was its creator. Such Socialism is regarded by Marxists as "drawing-room Socialism". The force of the description—regarded as a jibe—depends a little on the drawing-room. To have made Socialism a polite topic in the salons of the rich— to have made the term "revolutionary" almost one of praise—that surely was a more impressive achievement than laying dynamite in their cellars would have been. Fabianism, like Jesuitry, combined something of the wisdom of the serpent with the harmlessness of the dove. It is true, unfortunately, that discussion and good humour cannot accomplish everything. The mass-passions that explode in revolutions can be compared to temper in the individual; the great leader controls them, but he does not lose touch with them. It has been well said, Woe to him who stirs up the dregs of a nation. But the man who regards those dregs *merely* as dregs—or statistical items—leaves them to others to stir.

Shaw was never perhaps altogether a "leader", but he was—as Swift was—something of a demagogue; and he was also of course an excellent platform comedian. It is rare for a man of letters to be either; it has been almost equally rare for the demagogue not to be ignoble or for the clown not to be a little despicable. In this sense Shaw's importance as a public figure transcends that of all the ideas—some good, some not so good—of which he made himself the mouthpiece; and he will survive as a legend—it seems safe to say—when his controversies are as forgotten as "Wood's Halfpence". If today we can be "popular" and "amusing" without either condescension or sycophancy—if we can play the demagogue or play the fool without loss of self-respect—we owe all this very largely to Shaw: fittingly, to an Irish exile and a de-classed gentleman. More than any man of equal celebrity that there has ever been—more than Tolstoi, more than Whitman—he has made us feel that to be an aristocrat in mind and to be a democrat in opinions are not necessarily incompatible.

The Communist would assert, of course, that the Socialism popularised by Shaw and his Fabians among the British bourgeoisie was an emasculate counterfeit—a wretched near-beer compared with the sturdy Marxian vintage. But in one respect Shaw was the most consistent and logical of all Socialists—namely, in making perfect equality of income the touchstone of true Socialism. This Shavian ideal—like every other kind of rigid equalisation—seems to me indeed as undesirable as it is impracticable: undesirable because it would imply a state-control and mechanisation of life not to be borne (it could, for instance, hardly be applied without regulation of population)—impracticable because one cannot conceive of rulers who, apart from the rarest exceptions, would be content to receive no more than the meanest of the community. Indeed Shaw, in this matter, sometimes seems to argue in a circle: he explains, in his *Revolutionist's Handbook*, that the equal society will not come before the "Superman" comes, and, on the other hand, that the "Superman" can only be bred through the freedom of mating enjoyed by an equal society. Nevertheless it should always have been obvious in theory, as it is becoming more and more evident in the Soviets' practice, that Socialism with great income-disparity can only result in oligarchy—an oligarchy perhaps more despotic than any previously known; and it would assist clear-thinking if such "Socialism" were called by some other name, such as "Managerialism". The doctrine of approximate equality, as *one* ideal—among others perhaps more important and possibly conflicting with it—is to my mind irrefutable; and it would be strange if the intellectual classes, who have always been poverty-stricken, should oppose it in the name of a romantic gentility. In these days, a poet might be well pleased to be paid equally with a dustman; and only the thought of satisfying the requirements of a Board might make the proposition seem dubious to him. G. B. S. was surely right in proving that merit cannot be measured in material rewards—that such rewards vitiate indeed the very idea of merit; and that the man who is paid for his work is in fact working only for pay, as no artist and no gentleman does. In this sense he could cogently quote the Parable of the Labourers in the Vineyard, and the rain that is sent impartially on the heads of the just and the unjust. He is also to be praised for his contempt of the "Labour Theory of Value", that dreary muddlement which led Marx into such contortions of abracadabra—as if virtue could be weighed in pounds of sweat, and remunerated in the same proportion: a *reductio ad sudorem* of the Scholastic notion of "Substance", which still bedevils continental Socialism. Income should clearly in principle be equal, as votes and the right to justice should be equally distributed; though in the case of incomes this may not be practically possible without greater injustice. All that can be said for inequality is that it is better than state-tyranny, and the virtually greater inequality which such tyranny implies; possibly also (though this is more debatable) that an occasional millionaire is preferable to a million-headed mob. But those persons—whether capitalists or communists—who reject the idea energetically are moved certainly either by snobbishness or by greed, and they would benefit by reading the relevant chapters in *The Intelligent Woman's Guide.*

Nevertheless, since one may assume that there will always be some inequality, we should be wise to set one inequality to check another; and, I would modestly submit, there is a case to be made for a working landed proprietory, to balance the modern tendency towards a swollen city officialdom. Here Shaw, like all socialists—their eyes fixed on the abuses of a decadent feudalism—seems to me rather viciously urban in his thinking; agriculture, in his vision, was a matter for chemists, statisticians and accountants—and, of course, tractors. Shaw retained from his discontented adolescence—the four years which he spent uncongenially in a land-agent's office—an anti-landlordism worthy of the most virulent Fenian; and, to the end of his life, the Ricardian Law of Rent remained his chief Villain-of-the-Piece—its formulation, as a key to all economic ills, his proudest dialectical achievement. His denunciations of the Unproductive Consumer (slightly remote-sounding in the era of "Overproduction") tended to obscure the fact that the increase of leisure, not labour, is the true aim of society —that the rich are noxious chiefly as excessive savers, comparatively beneficial as educated spenders. He who delighted to expose the various "vested interests" in human ills—who talked sometimes as if doctors had invented disease and clergymen had hit on the idea of sin—failed to notice the most scandalous case of all, the interest of Banks in preserving scarcity; and one even suspects he would have dreaded a prosperity which should make an aunt-like direction by the statesmen superfluous. To the possible revivification of regional cultures through currency-reform he gave no attention; and by the whole habit of his mind, he thought of the nation as a counting-house rather than a country farm-house—a larger shop more than a self-supplying estate.

Shaw's deepest grievance against Private Property was, after all, its cruelty to the Well-Connected Poor. He felt keenly the resentment of the "downstart" (as he calls him)—the scion of a long line of younger sons, progressively pauperised by primogeniture. The hard lot of this unfortunate class—plunged from high living into low water—is more stressed in his writings than in those of any other sociologist I know. Ireland is still a country of large families and close family-ties; it is hard for the Irish youth to forget that his second cousin has an unworked-for "bit of land", and the remote possibility of inheritance is apt to put a break on all effort. In Shaw's boyhood there was in fact no recognised Irish "middle class", but only hordes of poor relations. G. B. S. certainly hated poverty more than he loved the poor— of whom he was wont to say, with gruff geniality, that he wanted simply to exterminate them. Almost the only really unpleasant characters in his plays belong to the class that Marxists call the Workers. Shaw liked no worker except the successful one—the sort of proletarian who becomes a dictator: the Mussolini, the Josef Stalin —who would seem to have appealed to him more even than Lenin himself. That is exactly the sort of proletarian whom less dynamic thinkers—myself among them—find it hard to like. In his aversion to the lower classes there seems to me something almost snobbish about Shaw. He speaks with extreme bitterness of his childhood-visits to the slums in the company of his nursemaid: "I hated these experiences intensely. My artist nature, to which beauty and refinement were necessities, would not accept poor people as fellow creatures, nor slum tenements as fit for human habitation."[1] This, after all, is not how a normal child feels; and the real artist is always a little attracted by the strangeness and the full-blooded life of "the people". It is the reason why the true artist can never be a really earnest reformer. Shaw's aestheticism was at the furthest pole from "bohemianism"; and it was not the least of his limitations that he knew nothing of *nostalgie de la boue*. In spite of the difference between coarseness and ultra-fastidiousness, his satire has something of the disgustedness of Swift's. His vegetarianism is almost the counterpart and inversion of the Dean's *Modest Proposal*—as perhaps his horrible "Ancients" are a variation on the theme of the Struldbrugs. His refusal to eat the creatures was due in part, one feels, to the fact that they reminded him of the "lower orders".

But Shaw, of course, was no mere orator and pamphleteer; though even in that character—I hope I have suggested—we should do very wrong to despise him. He also, after all, wrote plays; and if those plays tended to be discussions, they were discussions as dramatic as the Dialogues of Plato and as amusing as those of Lucian. He claimed, very definitely, to be both artist and philoso-

[1] Contrast this confession with James Joyce's *Portrait of the Artist as a Young Man* (see page 132). It is amusing to reflect, as I pointed out in *The Face and Mind of Ireland*, that Shaw and Joyce were not only fellow-townsmen but in fact namesakes. Shaw is the Scottish translation of the Gaelic *Seogh* (Joyce).

pher—and within certain limits we may admit his right to both titles. If he did not reach the greatest heights in either capacity (Ibsen was a greater artist, Schopenhauer a greater philosopher), he was perhaps truly great as the thing he called himself—an artist-philosopher—a Socrates who was also an Aristophanes. The man who wrote the First Part of *Back to Methuselah* (the only satisfying play in that series) certainly had the root of philosophy in him; and Shaw's definition of Life—the force that ever strives to attain greater power of contemplating itself—is an almost perfect one. He brought philosophy out of the universities and art out of the coteries—as he took revolution out of anarchist cellars; and gave needed dusting and ventilation to all three. As a philosopher he had an explanation of Existence, derived in the main from Nietzsche, Schopenhauer and (perhaps) Bergson; as that of Yeats was derived from Plotinus, Berkeley and Spengler (though both of them are under heavy obligations to Blake). As an artist he admired strong, vital, unmoral personages of all sorts and of both sexes. His greatness was that he put both philosophy and life upon the boards, and succeeded in fascinating us; but it was his weakness that he over-raionalised and over-moralised them both. His thought and his art, in fact, were never fused; it was indeed the whole mistake of his criticism of Shakespeare—and his misinterpretation of Ibsen—that he appeared not to know even the meaning of a true artistic fusion. More and more he tended—by the very force and honesty of his rationalism—to give all the good speeches to his "worldly" characters: the capitalist, the empire-builder, the inquisitor, the predatory female. And in so doing he made them (all except the predatory female) unreal.

Nothing could be said against him as an artist—it would indeed be his glory—if he had admired these types non-rationally, whatever the things they did and believed in. But he tended to identify himself with them—in his plays, and at last even in life—*because of* the things they believed in, or that he assumed they believed in. He was not artist enough to admire what he could not justify to his reason —and yet he was philosopher enough to *want* to admire everything that energetically lived; by instinct he remained a rationalist, even though with his reason he became a vitalist. In the early play, *Mrs. Warren's Profession*, a daughter has the better, in a "show-down", of her mother who is a brothel-keeper. In the later *Major Barbara*, a daughter is decidedly worsted and converted by her father, the armament-maker. Yet Mrs. Warren is a convincing personality, with some fineness, whereas Undershaft is too Shavian to be real at all. And it is not evident that brothel-keeping is more harmful than armament-making, though both may be necessary in certain stages of civilisation. Undershaft's arguments, however, are precisely the same as those of Mrs. Warren: that all are guilty under capitalism, and it is better to be guilty and successful than poor and "honest". (It is typical of Shaw that, while he afterwards said *Mrs. Warren's Profession* "made his blood run cold", he did not say this of the much more unpleasant *Major Barbara*. Undershaft—the ingenious sophist—was appropriately named.) In the same way, his two finest characters— Peter Keegan and Saint Joan—cannot divest themselves of a certain atmosphere of fatuity, almost of sentiment-ality; we are made to feel they are, after all, not "con-structive". Shaw was not a man without heart—as the philistines said—nor a man of second-rate intellect—as it has become the fashion among some of the highbrows to say; but there was a discord in him. It was not the unhappy familiar "split" between the senses and the spirit—for this conflict was not strong in him—but a discord between his emotions and his mind: a discord greater than the necessary contradiction which makes good drama. He was not integrated—which means that he was what he was always accusing everyone else of being: non-adult. He kept blowing out the "intelligence", like a boy with a paper-bag, until it burst. If he had written the Apology of Socrates, he would have turned it—even against his will—into an apology for Socrates's judges.

Shaw, we have seen, had something of Don Juan; but he had even more of Don Quixote. For he was always, in spite of the drabness of his conceptions, the essential nobleman—a grandee fallen among Fabians, it may be truly said. His very photographs vary between the laughing devil and the star-gazing chin-tilted dreamer. His quixotism may not be apparent to those who think of him merely as the "Anti-Romantic"; but he was a Quixote of the future rather than of the past, and he has never been appreciated by the realistic Gallic mind.[1] The Irishman—like the Spaniard—has both a peasant shrewdness and a tendency to unworldly dreaming; the Irishman who stays in Ireland becomes a petty huckster or a whisky-sodden poet, but the Irish emigrant—the "wild goose" of tradition—is capable of becoming a *conquistador*. The soft Irish earth is a bog for the feet of the weak, but can be the best of springboards for the strong; and the Irish mist, which so easily turns foothills into

---

[1] This is however in part no doubt the fault of the quite ludicrously inept versions of M. Augustin Hamon.

mountains, can lure and challenge as well as "damp" and depress. The boyhood of Shaw—the hungry and lonely youth, dividing his time between the land-agent's office and the heights above Killiney Bay,—has something of the boyhood of Raleigh. His famous "realism"—his appetite for crude and gritty fact—belongs really to the Sancho Panza side of him, but his Socialism remained to the end a Morris-like Utopianism, shot through with Carlylean hero-worship: a medley of sense and fantasy, taking small account of real historic trends,—the dream of a young Napoleon of the mind in a barren island.

For what was wrong with Shaw, after all, was an extraordinary dumbfounding lack of the historical sense. It is significant that he and his Fabians rejected the Marxian "historical dialectic", for that dialectic—whatever its faults—at least expressed the idea that Time is *Doom*, that there are deep half-understood forces at work in history. What Shaw said, absurdly, of Shakespeare was literally true of himself—the world to him was a great "stage of fools" on which he was utterly bewildered: he had no feeling for the *connèctions* of things. It seems a bold thing to say, but G. B. S. never realised (in spite of his deep study of Marx) the drive of *laisser-faire* towards imperialism and war—except, of course, in the general sense that Inequality of Income was the root of all evil. The Boer War (which he supported) and the First World War took him by surprise, as in fact the Second World War also did. He lacked even the prophetic flair of Mr. Belloc, whose *Servile State* (in which the capitalists would take away liberty in return for giving security) was a very exact anticipation of Fascism; but then, of course, if he had foreseen it he would by no means have been repelled by it. And in the same way his imagination stopped before the past. His Caesar professes the completest unconcern at the destruction of the library of Alexandria. "Will you destroy the past?" demands the scholar Theodotus. "Ay," says Caesar, in the very words of the *Hitlerjugend's* song, "*and build the future with its ruins.*" It is hard to see what future can be built out of cinders. Shaw's anti-traditionalism comes out amusingly in his impatience even with "old familiar faces". "It is frightful for the citizen", he exclaims, "as the years pass by him, to see his own contemporaries so exactly reproduced by the younger generation, that the companions of thirty years ago have their counterparts in every city crowd. . . All hope of advance dies in his bosom as he watches them." This frightful experience is certainly not my own, nor, I think, most people's: far from it. G. B. S.'s historical plays, even at their best, strike us a little as Christmas pantomimes; of these inventions it is, to a great extent, true—what is only intermittently true of his contemporary plays—that the characters are "gramophones". Or rather, while they are living enough, they live from no independent life—the navel-string connecting them with their author is not cut: in Caesar there is nothing of the Pagan sense of Fate, with St. Joan none of the intimate presence of the Supernatural, with Adam and Eve no feeling of the dawn of a world. *Caesar and Cleopatra* contains some of Shaw's noblest writing—attached to a dull historical charade, which might have been written purposely for Hollywood. Shaw's ignorance of the past would have mattered little if he had been a simple emotional being—after all, who cares whether Shakespeare's historical plays are "true to period"? But Shaw was as different from natural men as if he had been one of Yeats's "holy centaurs of the hills". The result of despising the Flesh is not that it makes a man spiritual but that it makes him mechanical —imaginatively *dead*; and a concentration on the mechanics of life is also, as Bergson showed, germane to the comic vision. G. B. S., who hated travel, had no more conception of an ancient Roman or a 14th Century French girl than he had of a 20th Century German or Russian. It is hard to forgive him his bouquets to Hitler; feeling, no doubt, that one Wagnerian must understand another, he could apparently forgive the *Führer's* second musical enthusiasm—*The Merry Widow*. And his film-star-like trip to Moscow—the story of the visit to Comrade Stalin, when the great man said severely, "But you *beat* children in England", and the plucky Lady Astor, rising like a tornado to the defence, "rocked the Kremlin to its foundations"—all this is merely irritating in its Social Column frivolity. In that world of ice-cold fanaticism—of terror raised to a consummate science—a world in which it might be said "Greater love than this hath no man, that he should inform the police of every word spoken in his hearing, no matter by whom"—a world in which tolerance, civilised discussion, all the free play of the mind, are unknown and proscribed: against that background moves a jocular old Irish gentleman—fêted, beaming and joking—seeing nothing at all—catching no murmur fainter than the "amplifiers" or deeper than the rustle of the snow—the perfect pedagogue-on-vacation, the complete Mark Twain innocent abroad. Broadbent, thou art avenged!

But the mention of Broadbent reminds me of the one play of Shaw's which really has atmosphere—almost indeed the only one: namely, *John Bull's Other Island*. The very topicality of that play makes it more real than some of his more ambitiously "imaginative" efforts. The Laughter Scene has a quality which we do not meet again in Bernard Shaw until *Heartbreak House*—something Dantesque, almost surrealistic. Even the remarks of Peter Keegan to the grasshopper ring less false than Shaw's poeticisms in general do; because the phraseology is that of actual Irish colloquial speech.

It is not quite the same with Shaw's other saintly character—St. Joan; G. B. S. had not *seen* her, as he might have seen the village saints and originals of his native country—he had only seen the excellent Dame Sybil Thorndike. In the play that bears her name, we find the following piece of dialogue between the peasant-maid and the Dauphin:

CHARLES: . . . If you are going to say "Son of St. Louis: gird on the sword of your ancestors, and lead us to victory" you may spare your breath to cool your porridge; for I cannot do it. I am not built that way: and there is an end of it.

JOAN (*trenchant and masterful*): Blethers! We are all like that to begin with. I shall put courage into thee.

CHARLES: But I don't want to have courage put into me. I want to sleep in a comfortable bed, and not live in continual terror of being killed or wounded. Put courage into the others, and let them have their bellyful of fighting; but let me alone.

JOAN: It's no use, Charlie; thou must face what God puts on thee. If thou fail to make thyself king, thoult be a beggar: what else art fit for? Come! Let me see thee sitting on the throne. I have looked forward to that.

It is not differently—or not very differently—that Dick

31

Whittington's cat apostrophises the future Lord Mayor in the pantomime. And the play continues in this vein—half comedy, half debate—almost right up to the unpleasant, very jarring, incident of Joan being taken and burned to ashes. We like this heroine—she is indeed nothing mystical, like Péguy's Jeanne, but a plucky intelligent girl with no nonsense—and yet there is little in her or in the world we are being shown to make such a horrible climax convincing. It is as if we were presented with Nancy Astor, cracking jokes with Stalin, and Koestler's Arlova, the girl-secretary of *Darkness at Noon* who was liquidated, as one and the same character. If we did not happen to know the story beforehand, we should look on the burning as merely a bad artistic fault; and because we *do* know the story, the argument and persiflage ring a little hollow—as a bright bit of dialogue at a dinner-table might fall flat for a looker-on who knew the food was poisoned. Suppose that Shaw had re-written *Othello* with the philosophical Iago for hero (and Iago was made to be a Shavian character). It might in some ways be as good a play—certainly a very interesting one —but the strangling of Desdemona would strike us as simply an extraordinary lapse of taste; the Aristotelian pity and terror would not form any great part of our emotions. After the first production of *Saint Joan*, there was a great deal of discussion among the critics as to the propriety of the Epilogue; but without the Epilogue, I think, the abruptness of the play's ending would strike us much more forcibly. Its purpose is, in fact, to restore the easy argumentative note which the intrusion of the brutal historical facts has a little disturbed. Yet nothing could be a more shocking anti-climax than this Epilogue in a true tragedy.

And yet there is real poignancy in *Saint Joan*, in spite of the rather brittle dialogue; not the tragedy of Joan of Arc—it needs an effort to remember that the play is about her—but the nostalgia of George Bernard Shaw. The hero who is laughed at, tolerated, petted, cannot conceal a certain envy for the heroine who is taken seriously and killed. Shaw knew only too well that had he been a fighting revolutionary, in many European countries, he might have suffered a martyrdom no less repulsive than Joan's; and the fashionable crowds who had delighted in his wit would not have raised a finger in his defence. I am not a communist, but Shaw was; and in spite of the pains he took to justify it, there is something necessarily a little ironical about the communist who dies a millionaire. Whatever one's politics, one cannot but be glad that the modern Socrates declined the hemlock; for martyrs are two a penny, and a great playwright is a prodigious exception. But we are touched that for once he laid off his slightly metallic self-assurance, and wondered—when he wrote *Saint Joan*—if after all he had made the better choice.

Full credit, of course, must be given to Shaw—and has been given him—for his sympathetic and "understanding" portrayal of the Inquisition—probably the most sympathetic one that exists in any literature (for Dostoievski's Inquisitor is not offered as more than a fantasy). Historically, it is doubtful whether the scheming Cauchon and his assistants were really nice men; but we can let that pass. That Shaw could so represent them is proof, at least, of how his mind had outgrown the rather crude secularism of his youth. In his preface he draws a devastating satirical contrast between the 14th

Century and the 20th—much to the latter's disadvantage!
And yet one is left at the end, of course, with the uncomfortable sense that there is "something more behind it".
Did not Shaw's conversion to the Middle Ages keep exact
pace, one asks, with the decay of libertarian faith in the
world at large—that despairing readiness to welcome
despotism in all its forms which has been so distressing a
feature of the last half-century? Is it not a sign of the
metamorphosis of a Fabian into a totalitarianist? One
has something of the feeling one had on seeing an attractive and persuasive Soviet film-version of the life of Ivan
the Terrible. Shaw's heart, of course, is with Joan; but
he regards her in the end almost as his Inquisitor does—
a charming child indeed, but a bit too much of a good
thing in the present world. Her last prayer, in the
Epilogue, is weak and sentimental: O God that madest
this beautiful earth, when will it be ready to receive Thy
Saints? Her enemies, who had quitted the stage too
hurriedly, would surely all have sighed "Amen". The
moral to be drawn from that is that *until* the earth is
ready for the reception of saints, it will be the painful
duty of the practical men and the guardians of order to
keep such foreign bodies out. Shaw may mock, but he
really sees no alternative; for you cannot have people
ruled for their good without an efficient police. To some
of us the growing power of police-states is as appalling a
menace as ever was the anarchy of capitalism; but one
remembers that G. B. S. wrote a whole tract (his Preface
to *The Simpleton of the Unexpected Isles*) to justify "liquida-
tions" and to hold up the Inquisition as a model. Joan
is a "sport"—almost a spirit—an anticipation of the
super-humanity which, in Shaw's biological vision, is
to replace man in an unforeseeable future. She is

an unhappy Trotzkyist—whose place, unfortunately, is before the Stalinist firing-squads.

I have dealt with *Saint Joan* at disproportionate length because it is perhaps Shaw's most important play, whether or no it is his best. (The difficulty of classing Shaw's plays lies in the fact that his finest works—*Candida*, *Pygmalion*, *Saint Joan*—tantalise us the most by their inadequacies, and only comparative trifles like *Androcles* send us away quite satisfied.) It deals with great themes, and deals with them well—whereas *Back to Methuselah* deals with the great themes rather abstractly and superficially. It is not perhaps (like Ibsen's *Ghosts*) a true tragedy, but it is a highly fascinating drama of ideas; for Shaw's admirable knack of "seeing both sides"—never shown to better advantage than in the Trial Scene—is in fact the comedic genius and not the tragic one. Moreover the portrait of the heroine, whatever else it is, is extremely sensitive. Shaw handles Joan with a teasing fondness, which reveals him as the old enchanter and cavalier he really was—an attractive side of his personality which we are also shown in his correspondence with Ellen Terry. G. B. S. could always draw a charming female when he wanted to, even if his males are over-afflicted with the curse of garrulity. Sometimes of course he did not want to, but deliberately sacrificed his heroines' charm to their intelligence: I think, however, that he did this less than is usually supposed. His success with female characters has been recognised by French critics (otherwise little appreciative of Shaw's work) more often than by English ones. It is too often asserted, even still, that Shaw's plays are only "disguised tracts", and his women mere "suffragettes"; but in fact the plays (all except the early *Widowers' Houses* and *Mrs. Warren's Profession*) are poor and incoherent considered as propaganda, and the heroines are often quite disconcertingly wily and feline. In all Shaw's major plays I can call to mind no revolutionists, except the scarcely-very-attractive brigands of *Man and Superman* and the housebreaker in *Misalliance*; for the eugenical-minded Tanner has certainly never even smelt a trade-union office. G. B. S. was not really a problem-playwright at all—either a good one like Ibsen or a bad one like Brieux; his true affinities were with the Anglo-Irish playwrights of the 17th and 18th Centuries—only that his world was a woman's world and not, like theirs, a man's, so that in the comparison he seems both more realistic than his predecessors and more prim. His art in fact bears much the same relation to the great Scandinavian realists as that of the Restoration dramatists to the Elizabethans; but he had the advantage that realism and the feminine wit are essentially more fitted to comedy, as romance and gallantry are the proper themes for tragedy. In *Man and Superman* the stratagems of Ann Whitefield almost (but not quite) console us for the sociological trumpetings of Tanner; she is quite evidently a villainess of the family of the Marquise de Merteuil, and a most unhappy choice for the mother of the Superman! Shaw's only fault, indeed, is on making her too blatant; it is incredible that even a fool like Octavius (one of G. B. S.'s worst failures in characterisation) should be taken in by her. In the downrightly sentimental *Candida* (which Shaw, meant, I suppose, to be his *Candide*) the heroine is so engaging that we fail to notice —and her creator himself seems not to have perceived— that she is a bit of a fraud. She stays with Morell, not because he is "the weaker of the two", but because from her viewpoint she would be making a bad exchange in leaving him for the poet—with whom she is not even in love.[1] She is not in love with him, and therefore the play lacks dramatic tension; and Marchbanks does not even want her sufficiently to put up any fight. Nor is Morell in fact—except in an extreme paradoxical sense—the weaker of the two; he is no feeble romanticist, but the type of a popular successful man. He would have quickly replaced Candida—as she well knows—by another capable and adoring housewife. It has been much discussed what Shaw really meant by "the secret in the young poet's heart". There is surely no mystery here—if we reflect that every Shavian hero is G. B. S. himself; though Shaw has certainly not made his point very clearly. He means that Marchbanks was to give up the Eternal Feminine (and poetry) and join the Fabians—the Fabians who were just one mental jump ahead of Parson Morell. Only on this assumption could Marchbanks have been (in the Shavian sense) the stronger man. *Captain Brassbound's Conversion*, again, which one would take from its title to be an uncompromising tract, is a play devised simply to glorify a charming and clever woman (specifically, of course, the divine Ellen Terry); it has no problem, any more than *The Doctor's Dilemma* has a clear-cut dilemma. It satirises, not law and punishment, but the private vendetta—a theme of slight sociological importance in modern Europe. The play would be morally superior if the subject were not Captain Brassbound's conversion but Judge Hallam's. And Brassbound's change of heart

---

[1] It might perhaps be said of Shaw and Lawrence—those two fine feminine psychologists—that Shaw could not show us a woman in love, whereas D. H. L. could not depict one who was not in that condition.

is really too rapid, unless we suppose (as, if the author were anyone but Shaw, we should naturally do) that Lady Cicely's feminine attraction played a part in it.

(I should mention, however, that I have perhaps been prejudiced against *Captain Brassbound's Conversion* by the prodigious difficulty of reading it—and it is likely that poor Ellen Terry was, at first reading, repelled by it for the same reason! Shaw has written nearly half of the play in the spelling appropriate to the Cockney character Drinkwater. It is a nightmare vision of what would become of the English language if it were spelled exactly as it is pronounced—by the majority of the citizens; and I have a ghastly feeling that G. B. S. would have wished to simplify our ideas like our spelling, so as to make them immediately apprehensible to every ratepayer.)

Arms and the Man suggests thoughts of the same kind as *Captain Brassbound*. It is significant that this—Shaw's single satire on modern warfare—should be his nearest approach to a popular drawing-room comedy: one might say indeed a bedroom comedy, for the bedroom scene—a traditional opening in plays about soldiers—certainly contributed to its vogue. The fact is (as we noticed in regard to the Shavian economics) that War was too grim and serious a theme for Shaw's handling—which is partly the reason for his failure with the younger generation, to whom War is a bigger fact than "Evolution". In *Arms and the Man* Shaw in fact satirises not War but Heroism, as in *Brassbound* he satirised not Law but Revenge—both of them typical Gilbertian themes, especially when the scenes are laid in Bulgaria and Morocco! In this play we may note the first symptoms of two dubious contemporary developments: the idealisation of the technician, without country or ideals, and the sentimentalism of the "small man". In Bluntschli, the chocolate-stuffing mercenary—"realistic", successful, but appealingly human—we see a first comic prefigurement of the modern military dictator.

One is reminded again of Stalin and Lady Astor, and gradually one seems to discover a pattern in Shaw's mind. Lady Cicely and the (converted) Brassbound—Napoleon and the Irish lady—Cashel Byron and Lydia Carew—self-made men of genius and divinely-wise society-women—why should these not settle all problems between them, with a maximum of efficiency and a minimum of excited unpleasantness: the pill of despotism (called by Shaw "philosophy") covered in the jam of suburban refinement (called by Shaw "art")? It is the solution which has haunted the literary mind of our time —assisted of course by the box-office, for strong males and astute females make "good theatre". A Socialist might complain—with a small grain of truth—that after the failure of *Widowers' Houses* and the suppression of *Mrs. Warren's Profession*, Shaw the playwright ceased being a social critic and became a mere entertainer—a romantic; those two plays, whatever their relative imma- turity and clumsiness, have a satirical force which he was never afterwards really to give an example of. Shaw the artist succumbed to the cult of the Man of Action— which is the artist's greatest intellectual temptation: for the man of action must commence as—in the demagogic sense—an *actor*, and if he does not lose his virtue (as Shaw did not), he at least tends to lose warmth of heart (as I think Shaw did, or he could not have been un- affected by the atrocities of the dictator-régimes). Shaw remained to the end, in a governess-like sense, a moralist, but he was not in his later life interested—as Ibsen always was—in personal problems and the individual soul: or the Undershaft-Tarleton part of him would not let him be. His personages tended even (as in *The Doctor's Dilemma* and *Getting Married*) to become mere burlesques. Shaw inverted, as it were, the development of Dickens; he gave up the social criticism which reveals character for the mere social mechanics which display "characters".

Yet, as if by way of compensation, if G. B. S. dropped the sociology—very largely—out of his plays, it became only more petulantly insistent in his other works. This is of course much to Shaw's honour; though I regret the great contemporary dramas he *might* have written, if he had not wasted himself between writing the mediocre *Back to Methuselah* and the blue-booky horribly-named *Everybody's Political What's What* and *Intelligent Woman's Guide*—between those tiresome cure-alls and King Charles Heads of longevity and equal incomes. In the last chapter of *The Intelligent Woman's Guide*, Shaw summarises his proposed reconstruction of society in the following harsh-sounding words:

> . . . I also made it quite clear that Socialism means equality of income or nothing, and that under Socialism you would not be allowed to be poor. You would be forcibly fed, clothed, lodged, taught and employed whether you liked it or not. If it were discovered that you had not character and industry enough to be worth all this trouble, you might possibly be executed in a kindly manner; but whilst you were permitted to live you would have to live well.

The number of bland assumptions, begged questions, dogmas and fallacies packed into that passage—and all of it launched at the head of a lady—is breath-taking.

It would be heavy-handed to enumerate them; and I
have quoted it here merely as a specimen of Shaw's style.
A little of that style can seem Napoleonic in its brusque,
military, business-like, brutality. Spread over innumer-
able pages, it is apt to produce the effect of a mad
Napoleon, incessantly marshalling and admonishing his
fellow-patients. Shaw wrote some of his finest prose in
defence of children against the tyranny of school; yet he
was himself, of course, of the race of the pedants. Head-
masters, because they never hear any voice but their
own, often develop the most fantastic theories, which
they are able to uphold with considerable caustic wit.
We have all of us met the pedagogue who believes that
capital letters injure the eyesight, or that boys can be
taught to do without most forms of food; and I believe
that not a little of Shaw's success in England came from
his conformity with this type—a type, oddly enough, ever
dear to English hearts. Nevertheless, the world of Shaw—
in which sex is a eugenic experiment that passion or
sentiment can only vitiate, in which work as such is better
than leisure or conviviality, in which liquidation at the
discretion of a super-police is better than imprisonment
for statutory offences, in which death means just "being
scrapped" and is in fact a very good joke, in which nine
tenths of the habits even of highly civilised people are
aberrations produced by capitalism—that world, when
you fully realise it, was not quite sane. The comparison
with Don Quixote, unfortunately, is double-edged. The
world has so lost its heart to the ingenious nobleman that
it always forgets he was, after all, not in his good senses.
Of what excesses would not a crowned Quixote have
been capable! And indeed there have been many such,
who are remembered with execration. While Shaw tilted

against such windmills as Inequality of Income, he was blind to the true "giants"—the ever changing shapes of ambition, pride and lust for power. Today such windmills—or windfalls—as inherited fortunes are less familiar objects of the landscape than formerly; but one might write over much of the world-map, like the ancient geographers, "Here be Dragons".

However, I come to bury Shaw and not to attack him; to try to "debunk" G. B. S. would seem indeed like a a parricide, for it was he who taught us the habit of criticising our elders—largely a healthy one when he started it, though Confucius would scarcely have approved. Moreover to attack Shaw is to lay oneself open to the suspicion of envying his success; as of course we all do, forgetting that, for the greater part of his life, his success was something more like unpleasant notoriety —the success of the clown which has in it always something of melancholy. During all my boyhood I never heard Shaw spoken of otherwise than as a jackanapes, a cheap and insincere sayer of smart things, incessantly putting out his tongue at whatsoever things are true, whatsoever things are honest, whatsoever things are of good report. It is possible that this alarming description of the man gave me a slight prejudice against him which has lasted, as it certainly inspired many of my contemporaries with a shocked admiration. But it was, of course, a very false description. Never has there been a man less cheap than Bernard Shaw. Never once did he descend— for the sake of applause, or any other reason—to the mean jibe, the unpleasant flippancy. In the course of his whole long, active and argumentative life, I am not aware that he once forgot his manners; indeed he did not have to remember them, for he was in an innate and

mystical sense well-bred. There have been few wits and
popular characters of whom that can be said; even such
a good-natured person as G. K. Chesterton had by no
means an unblemished record. To match his admirable
suavity one would have almost to go back to Socrates—
a character so much resembling him as to make one half-
believe in reincarnation. (And I am reminded that Leo
Chestov said, "Perhaps Socrates talked so much for fear
he should cry".) I am not so much impressed at being
told that Shaw was naturally a shy man. Of course he
was: all vain people are shy, when they happen to be
also intelligent. The point is rather that his vanity—
though tedious when it became a platform trick—was
never in the least offensive. The Smart Alecs may like to
claim him as their patron saint, but he was never one of
them. His literary style—discursive, erudite, and yet
swift-moving—reminds me curiously of Ruskin at his
undecorated best: Ruskin who also declared himself a
"communist" and "the reddest of the red". Yet there is
just this much of truth in the caricature; few great men
have had such narrow limits as Shaw—or (what is worse)
have been so unaware of those limits. An interviewer
reported to him a remark of Gandhi's, to the effect that
"all Shaw's writings have a religious centre". Shaw at
once became serious, sunk his chin in his hand, and
exclaimed—as if to himself—"That's true. That's *very*
true." This story almost makes me doubt whether
G. B. S. was really to be called religious, or even profound. A truly religious man, one feels, would have been
embarrassed at the compliment, and a profound man
would have been impatient of the triteness. To read
Shaw in bulk is to get a terrifying impression—a sense of
a mind utterly unreceptive and closed upon itself. He

really seems to have despised poets for not having "purposes" and great religious teachers for not having "programmes"; Keats, he said, if he had lived, might have acquired "something to say" and perhaps become as good a poet as Morris! Whether he was in earnest about the bouquets he handed himself is unimportant; but we feel that the indisputable superiority of Shakespeare—and Racine—was not unconnected with their well-nigh anonymity. It is true that Shaw sometimes went to equal lengths in self-depreciation; but a great mind, one feels, should be able to taste other great minds without the continual and meaningless comparisons which he indulged in. What would one think of Mr. Eliot if he were to say, every time he opened his mouth, "Milton had a commonplace intellect. I, on the contrary, . . ." or on the other hand (as Shaw said with regard to Tchechov) "I want to burn all my own works when I read Dryden"—just as if he were entering for a competition? The theological name for all this, I suppose, is lack of humility; but here again it is necessary to distinguish. Humility is too often a big word for thinking and behaving exactly like everyone else—or rather for not thinking at all and wishing to be taken as thinking like everyone else, and only acting as part of a crowd. I am Protestant enough to be attracted by the rare human being who thinks as he will (or as fitful reason dictates) and acts as he sees good and proper; and in this sense I have nothing but admiration for Shaw's perky independence. This sort of humility has become such a disease in our civilisation that I am inclined to think Shaw's wilfulness a greatly needed antidote. In the ordinary moral sense, Shaw was utterly unself-centred; he regarded himself as so much material to be used, and presently (in his

favourite phrase) "ruthlessly scrapped" by the Life
Force. But—and here is the catch—he made the Life
Force Shavian; he was on more intimate terms with it
than any believer has a right to be with his divinity.
Julius Caesar, as Shaw depicts him, is Shavian; Mahomet
is Shavian; St. Joan, charming though she is, is Shavian;
the sun, moon and stars, if he could get them into a play,
would be Shavian—just as Bulgaria, Russia and Ancient
Egypt are all alike Shaviopolis. Jesus he could not
Shavianise—He was too big for that—and so (in *The
Black Girl*) he made Him a little comic, and could not
understood that by so doing he gave offence. "It is the
doctrine that matters and not the man" said Shaw;
which meant merely that he read his own doctrines into
the Gospel, as he read his own propaganda into Ibsen's
poetic dramas. This is not cheapness in the mean sense;
it is what is called in Ireland "ignorance", and what the
Catholic Church calls "invincible ignorance"—a definite
failure in imaginative perception. Only Shaw's inferiors
in the plays are contemptuously allowed a separate
existence; he had none of those inspired moments when
a playwright—or indeed a non-playwright—can com-
mune with a being greater than himself. There is a story
of a lunatic whose fare consisted solely of porridge, but
who believed he was being served every day with the
most costly viands; "and yet", he used to say, "somehow
all my food tastes of porridge". So it is with the Pan-
Shavian flavour in the feasts Shaw sets before us. G. B. S.
was born in the heyday of the doctrines of Progress and
Evolution. He early lost his belief in Progress—though
more from impatience with the Present than from any
growth of reverence for the Past; but he clung all the
harder to Evolution. Like Aldous Huxley, he came to

believe in a new "mutation"—though one, perhaps, of a more energetic and forceful character. As theologians know, it is a dangerous belief for the soul: for it means setting something higher than the soul—higher, that is, than the mysterious unconscious part of human nature. Shaw, like Huxley, considered himself a mystic; but his mysticism never really taught him humility—just as that of Mr. Huxley has not yet taught him charity.

The plays which embody Shaw's religion of Creative Evolution are, of course, *Man and Superman* and the *Back to Methuselah* sequence. To all Shavians (and, I gather, to Shaw himself) these plays were immortal masterpieces, the Pure Milk of the Shavian Word, Shaw's true title to greatness and his testament to unborn generations. Well! I admire G. B. S. almost as much as I admire William Blake (which is saying a good deal), but this estimate, I confess, seems to me like Blake's similar infatuation with his "Prophetic Books", *Milton* and *Jerusalem*. To me, rightly or wrongly, these "Creative Evolution" plays are excessively tedious, except for their wit—and even their wit tends to be over-slick as in *Man and Superman*, or merely silly as in the interminable *Tragedy of an Elderly Gentleman*; they are immeasurably poorer than that tortured but powerful play *Heartbreak House*. I think them dull, not because they present a religion, and a religion which I personally do not hold, for the same would be true of the *Divine Comedy*: but because it is a religion which has never been held by any large number of people. It is in fact no more than a doctrine or theory—it has not mixed itself with human passions and motives, as even the belief in Progress did in the literature of the 19th Century; and in these plays G. B. S. becomes in truth a preacher—or, at least, a

facetious and prosy lecturer. To treat us to all the pother
about the Life Force, that we should be dragged through
Hell and the 16th Century, and for it all to end in the
very ordinary marriage of the talkative John Tanner—
this seems to me a real lapse in Shaw's humour, as does
also—on a more ghastly scale—the last act of *Back to
Methuselah*. The "Ancients" of Shaw's conception bear
no resemblance to saints, mystics, dreamers or thinkers;
they are just priggish, pettish, governess-like old eunuchs,
male and female—and their rasping platitudes rever-
berate through a world in which no sound of bird, beast
or human child is ever heard. Nothing could be more
unaesthetic than the Pygmalion-idea—which he here
presents seriously—that the perfection of art lies in the
creation of *living* statues; even though it gives him the
opportunity for some amusing satire of the living. *Man
and Superman* (except for the ever-delightful Scene in Hell)
strikes me as the most dated of the earlier comedies—
much less amusing than *The Philanderer* or *You Never Can
Tell*; and the enduring fascination of the Hell-Scene is
surely connected with the fact that Shaw is here using a
traditional symbolism—in however comedic a vein. Nor
is his idea of Hell as the home of the Unreal—in contrast
to Earth, the place of Reality's slaves, and Heaven, that
of its masters—at all a bad one: that is, if one excludes—
as to appreciate Shaw one must—any notion of *spiritual*
evil. By this allegory Shaw did not intend to outcast the
poets, *à la* Plato's Republic; at least I hope he did not,
though when one thinks of the idiotic Octavius and
Mendoza in the same play one cannot be sure! By the
illusions of Hell Shaw means, I prefer to think, those
flabby and meaningless conventions—whether of art,
thought or morality—which shut us off both from the

creative pains and the creative ecstasies; and G. B. S. saw "romance" as perhaps the worst among these labour-saving clichés. Personally I am willing to relinquish romance—with a few nostalgic sighs; though I might disagree with Shaw about the boundaries of that concept. The "romance" which means complacence in a distorted vision—whether of man or woman or country or cosmos—is, like a gold coinage, too costly a luxury to be safe or tolerable in our modern world. Perhaps, as we noted when considering *Arms and the Man*, romance is less easily exorcised than Shaw imagined; driven from the hero Sergius, it starts to shed its pink glow around the figure of the technician Bluntschli. Nevertheless the work begun by Shaw was a needed one, for romance belongs to an adolescent "wild oats" stage of human development, and we are today having to meet, as we can, its bills. It is my belief that the difference between the art and religion of the past and those of the future will be the difference between fetish and symbol, between illusion as *delusion* and illusion as fully-conscious "artistic license"; and in his service to this greatest of revolutions lies Shaw's real claim to the title of philosopher-artist.

But what is this? Is this not an admission that Shaw was right after all about his doctrine of Creative Evolution? Have I not in the end called him a true prophet? It is certain at least that to G. B. S. himself the doctrine seemed prodigiously important; and we owe it him to give it our very respectful attention. He thought—a little too hopefully—that it would be the religion of the 20th Century, and regarded it as that "synthesis of religion and science" for which so many slightly muddled thinkers are always seeking. Personally I would say that there cannot be a "synthesis of religion and science", because science deals in facts and hypotheses, whereas religion is concerned with symbols for intuitions; and while symbols (*qua* symbols—an important proviso) are eternally valid, hypotheses are by their nature approximative and changing. Thus the scientific part of Shaw's "Creative Evolution" was already out-of-date at the time when he advanced it, being at variance with two laws which the science of today—rightly or wrongly— accepts: the law of the Non-Transmissibility of Acquired Characters, and the famous "2nd Law of Thermodynamics". The giraffe craning its neck will scarcely explain all the variety of nature; nor have we "world enough and time" for the fantasy to be even plausible. Be that as it may! The idea of Superman is at any rate inconceivable, and its connection—in the *Methuselah* plays—with the theme of longevity (a comic motif which Shaw toyed with as far back as *The Philanderer*) reduces it completely from the grandiose to the grotesque. To me it is a sad thought that the artist who gave us *Mrs. Warren's Profession*, *Pygmalion*, and *Heartbreak House* (to name three quite dissimilar plays which yet all have greatness) could have written so many trivial garrulous pages around this nostrum of longevity—a notion fit only for H. G. Wells at his worst, and one in which Shaw himself—to judge by the buffoonery with which he handles it—would hardly seem to have believed. "Why do you fix 300 years as the exact figure?" asks the politician. "Because we must fix some figure" replies Shaw's evangelist, Conrad Barnabas. The Life Force, it seems must have it as cut-and-dried as that—just like a good civil servant, taking his orders from a Planning Bureau.

However, Shaw was of course serious enough about

Creative Evolution; and it will not do, in my opinion, to write off the philosophy of a great man simply as a foible or heresy. If genius does not mean having purer perceptions of truth than the common, then I know not what it means; and men of genius are, as Shaw himself somewhere said, the real "Apostolic Succession". When a certain belief seems to us to be meaningless—a belief which nevertheless has been held by better men than ourselves—it is most unwise to condemn it outright. Rather one should meditate on it as on some dark oracle of the Gods, and endeavour to translate it into one's own terms; for in these regions there are necessarily as many languages as there are men who think. It is thus that I approach, for instance, the doctrine of personal immortality—which (as it stands) conveys no meaning to my rationalistic mind. The difference between a man and a discarnate soul would seem to me greater even than that between humanity and the brute; such an entity as a soul separable from the body is to me unimaginable, and therefore—if it exists—not interesting. And yet I feel that the value and uniqueness of human personality—the permanence of the transient under the aspect of Eternity—could not, perhaps, better be expressed: that the religious myth (as I should call it) is the natural and fitting vehicle for the metaphysical idea. Similarly with this Shavian-Nietzschean notion of a new species which shall supersede man: again, an idea to me unimaginable, and therefore uninteresting. As it stands, it seems extraordinarily crude. Christianity's philosophical paradox remains for me irrefutable: the truth that man is higher than the brutes precisely because he can fall lower than they, and that a creature more divine than man would, as such, have the possibility of being more devilish also.

Only, of course, since such a creature is unthinkable for us, we could not call it either good or bad, or form in fact any conception whatever of its existence.

And yet it is surely not without significance that the call for the Superman should have arisen especially in this century—the century of greatest menace in history. As during adolescence in the individual, the *Will* in mankind has grown stronger than the *Instinct* of childhood or the *Reason* of the school; it must become conscious, self-assured and autonomous, or it will remain a mere anarchic "complex". Pagan custom and medieval-Catholic law have alike been superseded by a third, equivocal, protagonist—the Protestant daemon of Individuality. Humanity in the age of invention is the baby with the carving-knife, the beggar on horseback; can he grow up, with a jerk, before he cuts his throat or breaks his neck? "The overthrow of the aristocrat" said Shaw, with essential truth, "has created the necessity for the superman." If the democracy is to govern itself—and no alternative today exists—it must become an aristocracy; or to put it in slightly less unpromising terms, men must become—without any class-distinction—gentlemen. Mankind must undergo some great, still hardly imaginable, change—similar to the change it underwent when it passed from the matriarchal to the patriarchal phase; man as we know him is an out-of-date survival, like a horse-drawn omnibus. Clergymen may continue shriving him and wiving him, but unless he can become a better-adapted animal his doom is sealed; and it will not make very much difference whether he progresses forward, with the socialists, to the Red Terror, or develops backward, with the medievalists, to the Black Death.

That is the situation, and Shaw cannot be justly

charged with inventing it. It is after all unfair to blame his impatience, as if it were merely fussiness or pedantry; the depth of his disillusion with "liberalism" gives him, almost, the terrible greatness of Coriolanus. We may regret his welcome to the dictators, but his despair of democracy was not irrational; he knew the stupidity of our elections, and perhaps it was not his fault if he had never seen the savagery of a terroristic *coup d'état*. We may not be so attracted as Shaw was by the alarming vision of "an England in which every man is a Cromwell, a France in which every man is a Napoleon, a Rome in which every man is a Caesar, a Germany in which every man is a Luther plus a Goethe"—strange that he did not say, for greater symmetry, a Bismarck! For all that, the world of the Machine—the era of compulsory semi-literacy—demands a New Man, as it is already creating a New Architecture. I do not mean a man who is like a machine, but a man without the collective manias which at present make the machine deadly, who can keep the "machine" part of him—the analytic intelligence—clean and efficient; a man who puts his sheerly individual unmotivated instinct even beyond "Christian love"—love which has ended by producing universal hate: a man that—in their very different ways—both Shaw and D. H. Lawrence pointed to, with their similar, still rather bewildering, condemnation of idealism: but a man that Shaw (so much the simpler, happier, *lesser* prophet of the two) already largely *was*.

And perhaps the New Man, the Homo Shavianus, is already—here and there—being produced; and he is not at all a water-drinking tricentenarian like the grotesques of *Back to Methuselah*. The old England of Horatio

Bottomley is dead—Bottomley who was a perfect Hitler *manqué*—and it was very largely G. B. S. who killed it. Shaw might praise totalitarianism as much as he chose, but wherever his plays are performed there will blow a breath of humour, sense and urbanity—of all the best things that our age looks back to in the Augustan age. The New Man, I think, will not despise emotion as G. B. S. tended to despise it; but neither will he set emotion above reason, in the old fashion of the West. The free-souled man will no longer be regarded in the heroic-pathetic manner—as necessarily a rebel blinded by *hubris*, calling down the vengeance of the fates; for he will have discovered a new world of freedom within himself. Certainly one need not agree with Shaw that art and love are things that "evolution" will leave behind, or that sensual passion cannot be the stuff of high tragedy. Shaw would in a sense have been a greater man if he had been a weaker one, and if one could think of him—by any stretch of imagination—ending as Parnell did, or Lassalle. But if I were asked for one small instance of how Shaw has changed our world—very decidedly for the better—I could think of none more striking than this. When his play *The Devil's Disciple* was first produced in America in 1897 and in England in 1907, both audiences and critics, it seems, were non-plussed. Dick Dudgeon's declaration to the heroine that, in letting himself be arrested in place of her husband, he "would have done the same for any other man in the town, or any other man's wife"—this seemed, so short a time ago, to be a fantastic Shavian paradox, or a shameless attempt to pull the public's leg. Decent men, no doubt, had always acted as Shaw's hero does; but they had thought it necessary to "rationalise" their action by imagining a love-motive—until Shaw's laughter blew that particular cobweb out of human brains.

Again and again I return to G. B. S. for the sober tang of *reality*—as a dog will set to and make a medecinal meal off grass. He provides, it is true, no cakes and ale, but he offers us good wholemeal bread, and a milk which is really that of kindness—or at least of humanity. He is unfailingly genial without being sentimental—continually critical without being acidulated; we are never for a moment made to suffer, as we are by other men of genius, either from a fit of petulant spite or from an indecent assault on our emotions. He rescues us from the two extremes of cynicism and poeticism, in which the pure aesthete and the cloistered intellectual are always getting themselves bogged. His works are not quite art or philosophy, but they are *conversation*—and the best the world has to give; we go to them not to be inspired, moved or carried away, but to be interested and amused. We no more look for immortal beauty in his plays or final truth in his prefaces than we expect a pleasant woman to be a phoenix or a stimulating man to be a Solon; there is a pleasing amateurism about them, as about the old-fashioned booth and open-air platform. The charge that he gave us pantomimes or puppet-plays is not, rightly regarded, wholly a depreciation: he linked on, all unconsciously, with this ancient and symbolic art of the people! There is a sense indeed in which all of us are still not half Shavian enough. Even the most intelligent people, in their daily talk, fall into lazy assumptions which Shaw—if his ghost were to drop in—would set us laughing at in less time than it takes to say George Bernard: assumptions of sentimental optimism, of misanthropic pessimism, of class-superiority, of national self-righteousness, of sexual egotism and vanity, of pious humbug. Have I accused Shaw of some of these faults, in considering his socialist utopian creed? But how much did he believe in it, except as the more enlightened Christian believes in Heaven—as a standard to judge the world by? And for a modern copernican-thinking man, it seems more natural to project one's ideal upon the earth than into the sky. We may not like the Shavian ideal; but that is because of the contradiction—inherent in all mystical visions and utopian dreams—of attempting to represent abstract perfection in concrete terms. It is none the less healthy and proper that the attempt should be made. Plato knew well, as a thinker, that the temporal world of phenomena cannot be changed; but for all that he described an ideal Republic—and one which, if it were seriously endeavoured to make it real, would only turn out to be a totalitarian horror. At least Shaw cannot be accused—with our political "realists"— of preaching class-strife as the road to utopia, or trying to inculcate hate as a means of bringing peace on earth. He would almost have agreed with Daniel O'Connell that "the liberty of the world is not worth a drop of blood"—not, certainly, because of the blood, but because of the attitude which goes with bloodshed. When the famous Trafalgar Square meeting in the '80s was broken up by the police, the crowd turned to him for a lead; he told them sensibly to get home as best they could, and was content to be sneered at by half his friends for his lack of heroics. If we may think him over-tolerant of the sins of the Stalin régime, it was perhaps a little because he thought that criticism should begin at home, and that he would not pander to the English habit of self-whitewashing at the expense of foreigners; perhaps also because he remembered what we now forget—the infamous Tsardom which exiled Gorki and sent Dostoievski to Siberia.

.   .   .   .   .

I should like to end this essay with a grand peroration in the romantic manner—something like this. "And now, even while I write, the room becomes peopled with his multitudinous creation. Mrs. Warren, magnificent even in her shame, calls down the malediction of all mothers on the cold-hearted daughter that would condemn her; and the humble typist Prossy dreams of the socialist preacher, as the tiring-women of David's palace once sighed for the arms of the psalmist king. Hodson stealthily packs the pistols, in preparation for a journey to the interior of Ireland; and—after the secrets and revenges of Egypt have rioted and rotted around him— the colossal sanity of Caesar is acclaimed with swords." (Or did Chesterton write that?) "Dubedat, martyred by professional stupidity and pharisaism, utters the eternal Credo of the artist, while fingering the damp love-letter of a waitress; and Lady Britomart, strong in the unthink- ing pride of her caste, withdraws herself haughtily from the sinister jests of her husband the weapon-maker. Keegan, the village St. Francis, shares his sorrow with the grasshopper, and the warrior-maid of Orleans flings the undying challenge of innocence at her cowled and cowering accusers. The scene changes. We sit among gaping crowds in the Coliseum, when all that is sensitive and refined in a soulless empire is thrown as meat to animals; yet one spark of fellow-feeling between a victim and a brute topples great Caesar himself from his throne. Centuries pass; but man, the unchained un- changeable savage, still voices his immemorial cry for blood. We rub grimy shoulders, in a Western encampment, with bawling roughs, when Blanco Posnet—a wastrel but little superior to his fellow-wastrels—struggles and wheedles for the life which a single act of humanity will cost him. We are carried through unthinkable gulfs of time to the Second Eden: Lilith, the immortal Mother and Muse, reigns among her egg-born progeny—every woman an Edda Ciano, every man a Cecil Rhodes—who have replaced the linnets and lions of the old senseless wasteful unconscious Creation. They wander naked, through Model Housing Estates, discoursing wittily of mathematical problems. But, even as we gaze, their skin shrivels, their hair falls off, their eyes become sealed—they attain at last the bourne of Pure Thought. Pure Thought everywhere, and within it—what? It is enough that there is always an inside."

Apart from a slight element of parody (which I am sure G. B. S. would have been the first to pardon) that is how one thinks of the achievement of any other great creative writer. But, of course, one does not think of Shaw's work like that. His characters (except perhaps for those in *Heartbreak House*) do not haunt us in the least; they do so much less even than the monstrous creations of Molière and Ben Jonson. When all has been said of their gusto, their entrancing vitality, it remains true that there is something lacking in them, as there was in their creator; and what they lack is the sense of an inner tension, without which even comedy is mere slapstick—even if it is intellectual slapstick. The tension we miss in him consists in those wholly un-Shavian ideas—sin, temptation and remorse: or, in an older language than the Christian, in fear and pity—those emotions which the adolescent superman-worshipper will always despise

—pity for the unalterability of the human lot, fear of the forces which lurk under the most polished social surface. Even Darwinism was too stern and tragic for Shaw; he wanted a world in which nothing but temporary and remediable ignorance opposes the Will—in which there is no Evil but only Trial and Error. True drama may not necessarily be crime-drama, but at least it must contain darker shadows and more fundamental conflicts than Shaw knew of; and when the theatre departs too far from its religious beginnings it can only stage dressed-up theses—something a little thin and bodiless. In the earlier plays, I have suggested, the sense of guilt is given real and potent expression—as the sin of *exploitation*, under which all are born in capitalist society. But Shaw soon turned from the contrast of guilt and hypocrisy to the lighter one between reality and romance—he turned from satire to burlesque. To state it unsympathetically, his plays tended to become mere comic relief after the serious stuff of his prefaces—even if slabs out of the prefaces seemed sometimes to get incorporated in the plays; and when the plays themselves raised deeper and more emotional problems (as *Pygmalion* does), he got out of the difficulty—undramatically—by slapping on a post-script. What a play *Pygmalion* would have made in the hands of a more subtle ironist! But with Shaw it is only a piece of fun.

But such a statement would scarcely be quite fair. We should do wrong to measure Shaw against the Ibsens, Strindbergs, Gerhart Hauptmanns, etc.; his aim and achievement were different, and perhaps in the end more important. If he was not, in the traditional sense, a dramatist, he created a genre of his own—the dialectical extravaganza, the comedy of ideas, the very "feast of reason"—which, with the addition of new elements from the Subconscious, one can imagine as the drama of the future. It is no good to say, as so many do, "I enjoy Shaw's wit but I am bored by his ideas": for this is the same critical fallacy that Shaw himself fell into, when he used to say, "I admire Shakespeare's music but I despise his intellect". Shaw had every idea at his command for which an equivalent exists in the terms of the modern mind. There is today no rationalisation or philosophication of the sense of sin that commands widespread assent: which means that there can be no genuinely tragic art. The emotion of guilt has degenerated into the twin forms of puritanism and aesthetic diabolism: of both which perversions Shaw has been, by superficial critics, accused—charged by the artists with puritanism and by the philistines with diabolism. It may be argued that he is a horrific puritan in *Back to Methuselah*, in the contempt for the flesh shown by the Ancients; or that he comes perilously near to diabolism in his cult of the artist-dictator. These I think were weaknesses of his thought; but they were not distortions of his instincts, which remained on the whole generous, expansive and liberal. Bernard Shaw, it may be said, for the first time in our society made the Intelligence king: even if he exaggerated its capacities and over-simplified its tasks. With those great introverts and subjectivists—W. B. Yeats and James Joyce—we may proceed to a discovery of its kingdom.

    .   .   .   .   .

It has not been easy—this attempt to disentangle what I feel to be right from what I feel to be insufficient in Bernard Shaw; as he himself said of the Superman, it will always be hard to know just how much sauce to put up with from him, on the chance of his being right in the end! He struck a mortal blow at melodrama, both within and outside of the theatre—even the popular socialist form of it called the Class War. On the whole he did well, though we may wonder whether melodrama is not after all as necessary to life as mythology seems to be necessary to religion. I have said that he was the most nutritious of writers, and also that his world was not quite a sane world; the contradiction is only a seeming one—just as vegetables are the most healthful of foods, but consistent vegetarianism is a craze. He did not understand that excess is a part of health or that a sense of evil is an element of sanity; nevertheless, to an age drunk with romanticism he came as a healer. Partly for evil, but I think more for good, he has taught us to take politics less seriously—though this was scarcely his intention (only think how furiously Lloyd George once was hated—or Kaiser Wilhelm, or Shaw himself!) For when men have a lively sense of the absurd, they will not engage so violently in political quarrelling, and at the same time they will grow—unconsciously—more reasonable and humane. He admired the immoralism of men of action, yet no "leader" was ever less a man of action than he; and he deserved to be disliked by practical revolutionists even more than by capitalists. Unlike the German immoralists who talked about "romantic irony", he seemed to know, by an instinctive good taste, that immoralism is only proper in a sort of intellectual pantomime. Comedy, in the best sense, is a symbolisation of the life of the mind, the life "beyond good and evil"; as tragedy is an artistic selection from the life of action, which is the conflict of good and evil. Without endorsing evolutionary fantasies, we may say that man aspires ever towards that world of the mind—a world in which he can be both realistic Emperor and ironic Clown, both Player and Chorus. Our era has made such mental freedom, for the first time, a dim possibility for all men; and in that sense Shaw is a true prophet—a religious teacher of a new kind, but no less one than the sages of antiquity. He was a great man, and yet he was unlike any other great man there has been; as he himself said of his plays, he was *sui generis*. Either we are wrong in calling him great, or we must say that he was himself the new "mutation".

WILLIAM BUTLER YEATS

By Augustus John

II

W. B. Yeats:

MAN INTO BIRD

THUS FAR MY SUBJECT has been the most celebrated of all the artist-thinkers, but one in whom the thought and the art were never quite happily fused. I have now to consider a man who was unsurpassed as an artist and —in my opinion—valuable as a thinker, but whose art would not be the astonishing thing it is were it not so perfectly married to his thought. Contrary to the recipe (though not always the practice) of Keats, Yeats lived, when he did his best work, more by his thoughts than his sensations—even if his thoughts came to him under strange hieroglyphs rather than a conceptual language. Like the oldest philosophers he was a mythologist, and like the youngest artists he looked for his images in the "Collective Memory" of the race.

To this great achievement there was of course a reverse, which we shall have to examine. Speaking, as he so often did, of friends long dead—and including himself with them—he wrote the line "We were the last romantics". Bernard Shaw, looking back to his lonely beginnings, might have said, "I was the first Unromantic". Both men paid the penalty of their isolation. Yeats, after early youth, scarcely made a real friend; and he was content to exert little influence on the *Ideenwelt* of the 20th Century. He outlived everything except—a glorious exception—his genius; his verse, as he said, grew younger as he grew older. It seemed as if his mind became foolish, perverse and even crude; but through these very qualities he created for himself a solitude in which "Troy's high funeral gleam" might shine out the brighter.

As Shaw was continually called a mountebank, so Yeats was often called a charlatan, or a believer in charlatanry. And there was some plausibility in both descriptions. Only, as Shaw was content to be a fool for truth and a life closer to truth (as he conceived it), so Yeats desired only to be a charlatan for the purposes of poetry. Anything that would rescue poetry from being a mere Victorian schoolgirl's-album affair, and make it again a Mystery—a Priesthood! For that, he would be (so to speak) the conjuror spreading his carpet or the practiser in charms and talismans. And, like many who have followed these byways, he learned *some* truths which are not included in philosophy-courses—some portion of that ancient Wisdom which (as the legend of the origin of the Tarot relates) was given, for better preservation, into the keeping of the votaries of Folly.

It would seem as if there could scarcely be a greater contrast than that between the poet Yeats and the prince of prose Bernard Shaw—him whom Yeats said he once dreamed of (a most happy Dali-esque image!) as a smiling sewing-machine. And yet their lives and to a certain extent their characters, run curiously parallel. Both Irishmen had for background the exceedingly-small gentry: almost what in England would be called "lower middle-class which has seen better days". Both were Protestant in temper, in so far as they were anything (the real religion in which they were suckled alike was art); but they were as remote from anglicanism as they were from nonconformity. Shaw was utterly and

rather deadeningly urban, but there remained to the
end something "small town" about him, and he knew
the proletariat only as an abstraction. Yeats—more than
any writer of our time—had the Virgilian note of an
ancestral pastoralism; yet he had little real acquaintance
with country-folk or the country life. Almost his only
poem in which rural pursuits are mentioned—the hackneyed *Innisfree*—might be written by a pre-Raphaelite
who had been born in Chelsea. Both of them are first
heard of as members of the Morris circle, and imbibed
"infernal" wisdom from the proverbs of Blake; both of
them ended with a certain harking-back to the universality of Goethe. Both apparently kept their virginity
till near the age of thirty; both made happy, *terre à terre*,
socially very advantageous marriages, after long trouba-
dour-like romances which remained—whether by fate
or design—merely literary. (Shaw's coyness was a sort of
disguised attack; Yeats's ardour was almost a camou-
flaged retreat.) Both men were by nature timid and shy,
yet forced themselves to the drudgery of public affairs—
in which they revealed much astuteness and hard sense;
as Shaw was a vestryman, Yeats became a senator and
even a film-censor! Both of them ended as something
very like fascists—scorning the Mob, yet idealising the
Mob's leaders. Anarchical in thought, they were both in
practice almost too carefully law-abiding. Both were
dramatists, self-dramatisers, skilled public speakers,
failed novelists, in a certain degree comedians, more
"charming" than really likeable—and yet possessed of
that high single-mindedness which is the best meaning
of nobility.

This parallelism may help to explain that embarrassing
element of the charlatan in Yeats. It was, like the

Shavian brag and fastidiousness, in part a shield for an excessive shyness, in part the weapon of one who almost deliberately made of himself a myth. In a word—a word we shall meet with often in W. B. Y.—it was a *mask*: and Yeats talked like Wilde—though with a more hieratic meaning—as if the mask were more real than the face. But it was also something more than a mask—namely a poet's necessity to justify his faith, in a century of rationalism. Yeats, like Shaw, met many strange characters in the London of the '80s, and joined many strange societies; but I think that no one directed him so decisively towards the supernatural as his fellow Dubliner and art-school comrade, George Russell. What Sidney Webb was to Shaw, George Russell became to Yeats—an indispensable Sancho Panza. There was a time when it was usual to couple the names of Yeats and Russell, like those of Goethe and Schiller; but Russell today is even more unread than Schiller, and to the present generation he is known chiefly as a character in Moore and Joyce. George Russell (pen-named A E—the "Aeon") was a walking factory-of-poetry in ceaseless production, whose style may be judged from the line "Sounds the deep OM the mystic word of light": a muscular though mediocre painter—like a Corot in whose works the nymphs have half evicted the trees: a bombinating talker with a formidable shopman's-inventorylike memory. But I doubt whether he would have exercised the dominion he came to exercise in the Dublin of his time if he had not been something more remarkable: to wit (in the literal sense) a seer, a "visualiser". He *saw* the Beings which he delineated with his painstaking but insufficient pencil and pen. There was no doubt that he saw them: far from being a whimsicalist or playboy, he was one of those men—commoner, alas, then than now—whom no one would ever accuse of deliberate fraud. A cynic might have thought him, for that very reason, the more suspect; but in fact there was no occasion for cynicism. Persons endowed with this psycho-physical peculiarism certainly exist; they are not always necessarily saints or men of genius, though (like Blake) they may be something of both. Russell was scarcely one or the other, but he was a man of excellent intentions and versatile, though modest, talents. Yet to his diffident and enthusiastic friend W. B. Y.—dreaming of Shelleyan magician-princes, hating dogmatic Christianity only less than rationalism, seeking Blake-wise to restore the primacy of the Imagination—he seemed at this time a true Magus, bearded and helmed in ruby and gold.

It must be said that A E never descended to the vulgarity of the spiritualist séance. He did not need to; to him, as to Blake, the spirits (or whatever these phenomena are) presented themselves without being summoned. Whether Yeats also saw them (as he claimed) I will not attempt to decide. He certainly wished and tried to see them, and to that end became a séance-frequentor; and what he wished was soon believed. He had a craving for the Supernatural which was more than any frivolous curiosity, for he felt the very existence of the poet's world to be at stake. The man of imagination, it seemed to him, was either a "mage" or he was nothing. As Shaw saw the mere artist as a dweller in an epicurean Hell, so Yeats came to see him, Blakeanly, as a shadow among shadows, in "the glass of outer weariness, made when God slept . . ." and in *Ego Dominus Tuus*, Yeats compares the modern aesthetic aim of self-discovery (by which we have lost "the old nonchalance of the hand") with the self-surpassing dream of the saint or hero. Such a revulsion as Yeats's was common to poets about that time, affrighted by "materialism" and born too soon for the discovery of the Unconscious—placed chronologically, so to speak, between the rationalism of Shaw and the surrealism of Joyce. For them there were but two alternatives: to join the Roman Church, or to link on with the "Secret Tradition" of Europe—surviving from Pagan times and just then reinforced by a new interest in the religions of India. For the first, Yeats had too much independence of mind, and the drab methodistical Catholicism of Ireland could make no appeal to him. Therefore he chose the second. The same geographical isolation which made John Scotus in the 9th Century a belated Neoplatonist made W. B. Yeats in the 19th Century a Rosicrucian; and it is noteworthy that one of his heroes, the mystical Paul Ruttledge in *Where There is Nothing*, dies like Scotus—assassinated by his orthodox community.

What is this invisible—so-called "supernatural"—world, of which every man of imagination experiences "intimations"? If I may give a very brief and, some will think, very insufficient answer to this immense question, it is—I personally believe—nothing other than the sleep-world of the Unconscious: that sea which has encompassed man from his beginnings, but of which he has only in our day become aware—through the discovery of the limits of his conscious "daylight" Self. Thus every man contains, not only the archetypal family "trinity", but the related essences of all persons and things, past and to come; and the artist is the magus who can summon those essences to the floor of consciousness, by the holy power of imagination. The fault of all theologies —if understood literally—is not that they are irrational but that they are over-rational; they are abstractions from Reality, always interesting and—to a point— necessary, but apt to be more unreal than any frankly imaginative mythology. (And I would add, if theology is a false rationalism, "spiritualism" is a false empiricism, which seeks to build a religion by the methods of science.) The modern man in search of his soul (in the phrase of Dr. Jung) must, it would seem, reject doctrinal religion for the sake of quintessential religion; to express it in Yeats's customarily violent language, hatred of God may bring the soul to God. Orthodox Christianity— especially of course in the form of ethical Protestantism, but also largely as the rational synthesis of Thomism— has not the power to shock the modern intellect into belief. Such belief as it still inspires is too much like "wishful thinking" to supply a vital tension. For real belief there is need of what Kierkegaard called *dread*: Kierkegaard, who had in common with Yeats—if little else—a dramatic sense schooled by a father of almost legendary stature.

Yeats's reaction to the "supernatural" was always in fact chiefly terror, as his reaction to the "natural" was only too liable to be hate. In both these attitudes he has been subjected to a good deal of rather smug criticism. The critics forget that, in calling up images of terror (such as that in *The Second Coming*) he *feels* the affright that he conveys: and that his fiercest hatred is directed against hate itself, as in *A Prayer for my Daughter*—a poem often unjustly said to be merely snobbish. Nevertheless, it is true he abandoned himself to these emotions rather recklessly. It can be understood as the attempt to shore

up his religion and his romanticism, against the tide of a
levelling democracy; and also simply as the attempt to
inject himself in age with the vigour, as well as the folly,
of youth. Yeats gives a little the impression of an Atlas,
trying to throw off the weight of this too-too-solid world,
under which Shelley had melodiously expired. The
attempt is exhilarating—if a trifle ghastly—to watch;
but it was an attempt made at a certain cost to his
humanity. D. H. Lawrence, with all his Dark Gods and
his tantrums, was less isolated and spiritually barren
than Yeats. Persons endowed with a little more realism
and self-knowledge do not find it possible to dramatise
themselves as Yeats did;[1] they need no hermetic initia-
tion for them to find terror in the human predicament,
nor the support of a social caste in order to hate the
contemporary barbarism. In the Yeatsian temple the
priesthood really shuts out the laity, as the ghosts blot
out all sense of Deity (or as the Existentialists say, of the
Situation)—like those "clanging wings" which, he wrote
in old age, had "put out the moon": and the ghostly
dreams are rather more real than the priestly dreamers.
In his last phase, he seems almost like a spirit "sent out
naked on the roads" and seeking to reincarnate itself, or
like a player looking ever more hungrily for a mask. The
youthfulness of his best work is that of an old man who
had missed real youth; the fact gave him almost a spite
against modern poets who, dying young, had drunk of

---

[1] Yeats's self-dramatisation is quaintly illustrated by a passage in *Autobiographies*.
The poet—a youth in London—was taking lessons in French, and doing well; but
his father wished that his sisters might also join the class, and this proposal was
fiercely resisted by W. B. "How" (he writes) "could I pretend to be industrious,
and even carry dramatisation to the point of learning my lessons, when my sisters
were there and knew that I was nothing of the kind?" That is a very odd sentence,
when one comes to think of it. For Yeats, to be *really* industrious was itself a form
of pretending.

a wisdom beyond their years. And this was the cause
of the most regrettable incident of his whole life, as
posterity may well regard it: his exclusion of Wilfred
Owen and Isaac Rosenberg from *The Oxford Book of
Modern Verse*.

Yeats objected to the work of these most significant
writers on the ground that "passive suffering is not a
theme for poetry"—though he should have known, as
the translator of *Oedipus*, that this is a half-truth only
(and the work of Rosenberg can fitly be compared with
that of the Greeks). The sentiment of pity is not, as has
been said, wholly lacking in Yeats, though his pity—as
in the address to the shade of Robert Gregory during the
Black-and-Tan Terror[1]—is angry, challenging, bitter.
So emotional am I, I cannot read that poem without a
tremor; but I read such a poem as Rosenberg's *Dead
Man's Dump* with a possibly deeper feeling. Yeats's lines
are—in the best sense—rhetorical, histrionic; but there
is no impersonal *classical* pity in Yeats. For all that,
Yeats was partly right in condemning pity as a subject
for the lyric; pity is too diffused, too obvious, too moral
an emotion to be altogether a safe one for the artist. It
seems true that lust and even crime can spoil a poet less

[1] . . . Yet rise from your Italian tomb
Flit to Kiltartan Cross and stay
Till certain second thoughts have come
Upon the cause you served, that we
Imagined such a fine affair:
Half drunk or whole mad soldiery
Are murdering your tenants there,
Men that revere your father yet
Are shot at on the open plain.
Where may new married women sit
And suckle children now? Armed men
May murder them in passing by
Nor law nor parliament take heed.
Then close your eyes with dust and lie
Among the other cheated dead.

than humanitarianism can; for lust and criminal instincts are sharp and shattering experiences—they have power to shake a man out of his gregarious self-esteem. Nevertheless if the poet be big enough, and if the occasion be big enough, pity can strike the true spark out of him—because it can move him more, perhaps, than anything else could do. Thus Oscar Wilde's best poem is *The Ballad of Reading Gaol*; and one may sometimes wish that Yeats (under the persuasions, perhaps, of Maud Gonne) had at least once gone to prison! There are finally only two ways open to the poet of writing about modern war—the contemplative way of Wilfred Owen and the adolescent "heroic" way of Rupert Brooke; and W. B. Y., if he had been English, would have written like Brooke rather than like Owen. Yeats, it is true, suggested a third way (in the Preface to *The Oxford Book*)—the gallows-humour of the Irish street-ballad "O Johnny I hardly knew you"; but that surely would be an absurdly inadequate manner of treating Armageddon.

The place of abstract thought in verse, and in the verse of Yeats, is somewhat similar to that of moral emotion. It was well said by Goethe that the poet must have philosophy, but he must keep it out of his poetry—meaning, of course, under the surface of his poetry. I have actually seen it stated, by critics in a state of indignation with his "fascism", that Yeats was a self-indulgent trifler, a "decadent" without heart or mind. Actually there was almost too much human emotion in Yeats—though emotion of a private and personal sort; and he possessed a rather too tight and systematic philosophy. It is possible that posterity may be less interested in those friends whom he is never tired of celebrating; and it is doubtful if the theories of *A Vision* will ever receive the consideration they certainly deserve. We are unlikely to see a time when that book will form part of any school syllabus, and I do not know a single critic who has written about W. B. Y. without thinking it necessary to apologise for it;[1] yet I cannot see why it is the less a contribution to philosophy, simply because Yeats wrote well and because he did not disdain traditional myth—considerations which would equally exclude Plato were he alive today. If the critics admit Plato to be the greatest of philosophers in spite of the *Timaeus* and the *Phaedo*, and yet refuse to take Yeats seriously, it is because they invoke some unexamined dogma of "progress", and feel that a 5th Century pre-Christian Athenian has licence to believe many things which are forbidden to a 20th Century Irishman. But this is to treat philosophy, in the modern manner, as a mere filing-system for the sciences, instead of—as it should be—a "vision of reality", the reflexion of the universe in a mind: and it is also to ignore the most recent tendencies—looking back to Plato—in psychology and anthropology. The fact that the doctrines of *A Vision* were given (through Mrs. Yeats) in automatic writing, ought surely not to prejudice us either for or against them—any more than our judgment of *Kubla Khan*, as poetry, is influenced by the fact that it was written in a trance; and in fact the kernel of the Yeatsian system was

---

[1] It is customary to excuse *A Vision* as a "scaffolding" for Yeats's later poetry; but it should be clear that unless a scaffolding is founded in reality, the edifice will not be well-built. Any system of abstract thought, to have any worth, must be in the same sense a scaffolding—if not for the philosopher's own creative work, then for the art and concrete expression of other men. Thus Thomas Aquinas's *Summa Theologica*—as well as being, in a certain sense, a poem in its own right—was the scaffolding for the *Divina Commedia* and for a great part of the art of the Middle Ages. Our art today tends to be personal because our philosophies are personal.

contained in *Ego Dominus Tuus* and other poems, for which this unusual origin is not claimed. It seems that Yeats's terms—tinctures, gyres, etc.—are mirth-provoking for the average season-ticket holder; but when a famous philosopher, now dead, wrote of "concrescence" and "prehensions", there is nothing in that to shock. In its general lines, *A Vision* has affinities with Hegel's Philosophy of Spirit, though Yeats has in some ways a more worthy conception of personality than Hegel had; for Yeats as for Hegel, all things are from thesis and antithesis, and a phase is not negated (as Yeats supposed that Hegel taught) when it passes over into its opposite. I will quote here but one sentence from that work, among the many suggestive sentences it contains: a thought which I imagine would mean little enough to most of the professors ("Lord what would they say . . .") but which, for anyone to whom philosophy is still in the Greek sense a *theoria*—a meditation—would, I think, disclose a wealth of meaning:

Christ mourned over the length of days and the unworthiness of man's lot to man. His predecessor mourned over the shortness of days, and the unworthiness of man to his lot.

I am no initiate of arcane schools, and I cannot tell what Yeats meant by these words; after all, as W. B. Y. himself once said, "If an author interprets a poem of his own he limits its suggestibility—you can say it means . . ." this or that. The antinomies of Man the Doer and Man the Sufferer—the misery of Death and the perhaps greater oppression of Eternity—the truth that every age has its divinity or "daemon", and that that divinity is the self in man which knows and mourns

—mourns that he is worthy to die, mourns that he is unworthy to die—the eternal love-hatred between man's inner contradictions, his gay and bitter alternations of pride and humility: all this and more would seem to be contained in it, like the tree Ygdrasil in a flying seed. And to those critics who will object "When did Christ so mourn?"—"Show us your evidence"—"Did you read it in Babylonian cuneiform inscriptions?"—"To what Predecessor do you refer?"—"Can your remark be put in the form of a meaningful proposition?"—"Confess, sir, that you have treated us to a bit of beautiful poetical bletherskite"—to them there is really nothing to be said. They have never looked "out of the eye of a saint or out of drunkard's eye"; and we must leave them to go on repeating that Yeats was an excellent poet certainly, but not (like Mr. Dewey and Professor Babbitt) a Thinker.

Still, W. B. Y. could be exasperating enough as a thinker, and even a little more oracular than a poet should be. His thought, being poetic, tended to be rank; and his poetry, when it was philosophic, was apt to resemble an incantation. Yeats was a symbolist in the technical sense of a man using sounds and word-associations to express moods, and also in the more usual sense of one who employs images to represent ideas: the first is the process of dream, the second that of metaphor —to use Coleridge's terms, they are (roughly) fancy and imagination. In the finest poetry, no doubt, the two types of symbolism concur; and Yeats deserves credit for asserting a connection between them, half a century before the school of Jung established it. But Yeats was too apt to substitute the one kind for the other, by a half-conscious sleight-of-hand. And this is complicated by the irritating "magical" use of symbols as a sort of passwords, not to reveal but to conceal—a proceeding which has nothing poetic, but suggests the rather grubby schoolboyism of "masonry". The result is that, regarded as "fancy", the verse often seems slightly portentous—as "imagination" it is sometimes apt to seem bogus. Thus one is a little wearied, in the early Yeats, by such hoitsy-toitsy poeticisms as that he has been "changed into a hound with one red ear" (none the better because the poet may have believed in such a transformation); and the mood and image of *The Second Coming* are like a reminiscence of Shelley's *Ozymandias*, conflated with the Sphinx. Just as Yeats's emotions hardly extended further than a few friends (mostly dead), so his thoughts moved in a "golden net" of symbols that shut out much of the real world: elsewhere he compares them, truly enough, to mummy-cloths. One of the claims of occultists is to be able to produce phantom flowers; but one may per-haps be pardoned for preferring real flowers—those flowers which Yeats has so rigidly excluded from his poems. Nor is it only flowers that one misses there! It has been remarked that nowhere in the works of Nietzsche will you find mention of a machine; and the same could be said of Yeats. The dismal goings-on at séances meant more to him than war, industry, economics, navigation, the not wholly-uninteresting modern urban scene—more even than the Shepherd's Calendar. The tireless experi-mentalism of Yeats's craftsmanship—and his accurate ear for the rhythms of Irish speech—partly conceal the *bookishness* of his content. His symbolism verges on that lesser thing, allegory—or at least emblematisation; the fact is disguised by the unfamiliarity (to most people) of the images, drawn from esotericism or the Irish sagas.

When, in fact, his poetry is truly inspired his images are often enough classical, and even hackneyed—Leda and the Swan, Helen and the topless towers of Troy, Oedipus and the Sphinx; for the Gaelic mythology had been exhumed, unhappily, too late to take on new life. Here indeed he achieves the feat of filling the old bottles with the wine of modern reality; but it is after all such a very small part of that reality. And, owing to the tightness of the system, Yeats's stock of images is very limited; only for the perfection of the art they would quickly become monotonous. He achieves his effects, very often, in the rather maddening Gertrude Stein manner—by the recurrence of a single word, like the beating of some savage gong. The animals with which he fills his poems suggest heraldry rather than nature (I would like to ask, do ravens "stand and sniff the wind"?).[1] They tend to be always the same animals: that is to say, they tend to be *birds*—especially such birds as herons, swans, parrots (preferably green), gulls (sometimes man-headed), hawks (whose movements Yeats studied, with intensity, in the Zoo),[2] etc. (But it would cause us mild surprise to come upon a *chaffinch* in a Yeats poem—except indeed in the very early, nowadays over-neglected, Yeats. The poet of *Crossways* was himself, in after-life, a little of a "Stolen Child".) After being deafened, in poem after poem, with the clanging and whirring of wings—as if an aviary had got loose in the verse—one feels that ornithological rape has been committed, not only on the hapless

---

[1] *The Two Trees* (which, in the later versions, contains this phrase) is one of the poems which have suffered most from Yeats's itch for re-writing. It is hard to admire the spectacle of the Loves "gyring, spiring to and fro". One is reminded, a little unhappily, of *Jabberwocky*—a monster who has more kinship with the daemon of Joyce: ". . . the slithy toves/Did *gyre* and gimble in the wabe".

[2] Hone, *Life*, p. 308.

77

Leda but on the unhappy reader.[1] Yeats's art might be compared, unsympathetically, to Madam Blavatsky's cuckoo, which, when he made his first call upon the formidable lady, came out of a broken Swiss clock and hooted at him! Birds are all very well, but few experiences can be so unnerving as to find oneself in a closed space with one—and that is exactly the feeling one receives, and is meant to receive, from such a poem as *The Mother of God*. Yeats writes about birds, that is to say, because they are terror-inspiring—bringing to mind Meredith's "Eye and have, my Attila". That, however, is only one aspect of a bird, and not the most interesting one,—as it is only one aspect of the Annunciation.[2]

Bernard Shaw said somewhere that if the Life Force had been aiming at Beauty it would have stopped—Aristophaneanly—at the birds. He forgot that the birds have not yet, like the pterodactyls, been thrown on the scrap-heap, and they will very probably outlast the humans. But the point is rather that, while a bird can create—or at least utter—a song (for the birds are executants and not composers), it takes a man to create a bird—such as the emperor's golden bird of *Sailing to Byzantium*. Shaw's evolutionism leads in fact to much the

[1] It is said that Yeats once was asked to adjudicate on whether "swans" or "birds" produced the happier effect in the last line of a certain famous limerick. Students may be interested to know that he plumped decisively (and with great seriousness) for "birds".

[2] In Yeats's thought the Virgin Mary is at one moment Leda, at the next Leda's offspring, Helen of Troy—the "fierce virgin" through whom came the destruction of the old civilisation. Helen is of course also associated with another fierce virgin—Maud Gonne—who, indirectly, brought ruin on the Great Houses in Ireland. With Yeats (as with Shaw) the male is usually passive in the sex-relation; when the female is given the passive role, the male has to be metamorphosed into a bird—which again, by another shift in the play of symbols, carries suggestions of the Phoenix-like Maud. (And one remembers that Maud Gonne always used to travel with "cages full of birds . . . and once a full-grown hawk"—*Autobiographies*.)

same conclusion as Yeats's aviolatry—to a worship of disembodied force; and one recalls the oviparous super-humans of *Back to Methuselah*. It is treason to an artist's faith to suggest that the Life Force is not aiming at Beauty (and nothing but that); still, one feels a connection between Yeats's very un-artist-like interest in spirits and his dubious cult of the sub-human. The seers of the Middle Ages said the Coming of Antichrist would coincide with the end of the 2nd Millennium A.D., and would precede the true "Second Coming" by a short interval (an idea which Jung-students will understand if it be translated into terms of the "Shadow" and the "Anima"); and it has always been a tendency of the looser sort of mystic to get these events mixed up. There is a truth—the truth which Bernard Shaw and his like have missed—in the allegory of Leda, in the Centaur image, the Sphinx image; it is true that the civilised must be rejuvenated by the primitive, and that the Christian legend has led to undue depreciation of the physical. It is true perhaps, as Synge once said, that before poetry can be human again it must learn to be brutal. Nevertheless, the images of Leda's Swan and the burning roof of Troy are apt, for a contemporary reader, to start a different train of associations. One thinks inevitably of our iron dragons of the air, and the destruction of Guernica and Warsaw: not, in fact, of a refertilisation of the sophisticated by the natural, but of the complete annihilation of nature by science. Yeats draws tragic zest from the thought of King Priam "confronting murderous men", but such dramatisation merely mocks—by its unaptness—the sorry ending of his friend Kevin O'Higgins, to say nothing of wider misfortunes. The youth of Europe, accustomed to lifting up their eyes to the heavens from which shall come their ruin, would not, one fears, read Yeats with complete sympathy. *Leda and the Swan* is a great poem, but the conception is too inhuman to produce great drama. It could bring forth only *The Herne's Egg*.

But the mention of that puckish fantasia reminds us that we should be wrong to take Yeats too tragically. His mind has the gaiety, as well as the bitterness, of a player's mind; and his universe of "gyres" is a sort of cosmic roundabout. Like that scarcely inferior artist, his painter brother Jack B. Yeats, the travelling-shows of his West-Country youth seem to have exerted a lasting fascination over him. As he revealingly says,

> Players and painted stage took all my love,
> And not those things that they were emblems of.

Such a world as Yeats's is necessarily a highly stylised one; but an idealist philosopher cannot affirm that it lacks relative truth—especially when, like the Yeatsian "Vision", it imposes itself powerfully on the imagination. The "visions" of a true poet, that is to say, operate the translation of the eternal Forms into temporal Fact—when the visions are truly inspired and the Forms really "portions of Eternity". Nor perhaps should we forget the element of humour or mere wilfulness in Yeats—a Platonic idea or daemon for which philosophers (like the king in the tale of the Sleeping Beauty) too often omit to set a plate at their feasts of reason. Yeats—as if to guard himself against an unimaginative literalism—almost invariably mixes humour with his weightier speculations; and *A Vision*, though of course serious in its central thought, contains a high proportion of that saving

quality.[1] One need only recall the story of the philan-
thropist who—ineffectually, alas,—devoted his life to
teaching cuckoos to make nests; or (in another book) the
Cabbalist Yeats visited who "spent the day trying to look
out of the eyes of his canary, and announced at nightfall
that all things had for it colour but nothing outline".
(His method of contemplation, Yeats comments, was
probably in error.) Similarly the poem *Sailing to Byzantium*, which has greatly exercised the commentators, is
not without a certain pleasing absurdity. That the
immortal part of W. B. Y., on quitting its house of clay,
should be carried back through the centuries and enter
into a mechanical bird, designed to amuse the leisures of
a sleepy Byzantine emperor—that is a fancy which might
well make the "soul clap its hands and sing and louder
sing"; and there is another twinkle in the Keatsian aside
"Those dying generations". Not indeed that *Sailing to
Byzantium* is mere whimsy. It is a philosophical fable for
the poet's self-perpetuation in his verse, and, again, for
the reintegration of the fragment Man in the cosmic
Pattern: that great Pattern which yet, for its Artificer-
King, would be small—like a toy-tree with toy-birds in
its branches. One does not need to "believe" in magic or
metempsychosis to find this poem a deeply significant
one.

It is usual to compare the Byzantium poem which
opens the volume called *The Tower* with the more cloudy
but perhaps even more splendid *Byzantium* in *The Winding Stair*. The second poem differs from the first in being

---

[1] Yeats was too much of a romantic to be really humorous, but he enjoyed the
"romantic irony" of ambiguity and equivocation. He was even something of a
practical joker (and could be guilty of the slight tastelessness inseparable from
practical joking); for the practical joke partakes in the theatrical concept of "gay
tragedy" or "character isolated by a deed".

more impersonal. Here the poet is no longer *sailing to* the holy city—entering into occupation of his tower. He has made that symbolic step, representing his passage from youth to age—as also the change to a new sort of poetry, more subjective and more subtle—and he now writes as a night-walking inhabitant. The verses have a greater abstraction; we are with Shelley rather than Keats, and the contrast between the "many-coloured dome" and the "white radiance" is the motif—a radiance which suggests, to an Irishman, the wild and gusty Irish light. Even the metal bird has lost some of its solidity, and becomes more patently a symbol; it is assimilated to those cocks of Hades which crow upon the soul's rebirth —which crew, in *Solomon and the Witch*, "three hundred years before the Fall", and never again till Chance became "at one with Choice" in the perfect nuptials. The country of the young has receded from the picture, and its place is taken by a dolphin-torn sea (the dolphin —emblem of the dual nature of love) almost lapping the imperial pavements. We call to mind the progress of the poet from the Faery of his early pagan dreams, through the "Galilean turbulence" of manhood's passions, to his later hard and gem-like intellectual flame: the three meanings, it might be said, of his favourite Tower-symbol—the aesthete's Ivory Tower, the Phallic Tower which is also a Cross, the star-pointing Tower of the sage. The magus has come into his own—Artifice and Artificer in the end are one—the Dreamer's death-in-life, as he drew an Image of Beauty from the shades, has turned into the Knower's life-in-death, of sight and unterrified acceptance: the lost Gaelic Atlantis had become—for one superb instant—a modern man's "Byzantium Regained".

Yeats could not of course maintain this magnificence continually; though he achieved it fairly often, as in the wonderful *Supernatural Songs*. Those poems, like *Byzantium* itself, are very physical as well as being very metaphysical;[1] but the opposites are held in a tension which gives the verse its peculiar knotted strength. In other poems the sea of physicality not only laps the Emperor's pavements but submerges them, as the waves overwhelmed Cuchulainn; that hero who fills Yeats's imagination almost as much as Helen of Troy, and who —like her—was begotten by a bird. The coarseness which appears in *A Woman Young and Old*, the *Crazy Jane* songs, and elsewhere, is too easily dismissed as an old man's salacity; actually many of these poems are as sensitive in their feeling as they are subtle in their technique. D. H. Lawrence should have approved of the later Yeats: for Yeats achieved triumphantly the effect that Lawrence—in his verse—aimed at, but too often marred by his prophetic stridency. (And Yeats put the whole of the Lawrentian philosophy in a sentence when he said, "Our bodies are nearer to our coherence because nearer to the 'unconscious' than our thought.") Yeats's sexual poems are coarse in the plain 18th Century manner, but they have neither the disgustedness of Swift nor the prurience of Sterne; there is no jibing at the woman—or, where there is, it is balanced by the jest against the man, and both have their intellectual point. Some might indeed complain that they have too much "point", as though it was attempted to compress Browning's dramatic monologues into roadway songs:

[1] Yeats was descended on the maternal side from maritime traders, and *A Vision*, with its many diagrams, has the pleasant *physical* feeling of an old-fashioned sea-captain's log-book.

"the joints of Heaven crack" under Yeats's attempt to turn the Muse into a Sybil—he gives us a little the impression, I will not say of a diminutive Michelangelo, but of a Michelangelo turned miniaturist. Yeats was not the inverted Puritan—and if he became indeed an inverted Romantic, the inversion was conscious and deliberate, and therefore had no smell of the pathological. In Ireland, precisely because the situation is uncomplicated either by feminism or a *religion d'amour*—because the freedom of love, like the freedom of thought, is outlawed there—, the true relation between the soul and the senses which the world seeks may perhaps grow, like a rose amid rock and thorn. The Irishman, who fears passion, may discover its secret; because he has guarded (even if in a negative sense only) the old religious awe of the body, he is safe alike from sticky sensualism and the beautiful reasonableness of the modern lecture-rooms. Hatred of Eros can bring the soul to Eros.

Yeats, I have suggested, must appeal powerfully to all those who are, as he was, solitary in their souls; and his solitude—like that of some wandering sea-bird—is not at all morbid, but has fire and zest. Yet one rather doubts if he will ever be a popular poet—even in the sense in which he once dreamed of being one. His expression—in his later work—is almost perfect within its own terms: but the terms are too unfamiliar, remote and chilly to mean much to ordinary men—even to ordinary cultivated men. There is little hint in his work of living people, or the living earth; the poet might almost be a denizen of the Moon—that Moon by whose shadows he counts the steps of his dialectic. (It is significant that *A Vision* divides history into light and dark Moon-phases—not, like the very similar conception of Spengler, into noons and nights, summers and winters.) He can write, it is true, of "Urbino's windy hill": but that means after all nothing, for every hill in Yeats's verse is windy, and there is more dramatic precision in the phrase of Synge's Christy Mahon—"a windy corner of high distant hills".[1] Even the coarseness suggests a peasants' *Kermesse*, seen by a nostalgic traveller who would be most uncomfortable in the hurly-burly; and in his lingering over perished grandeurs he has the sentimentality—masked by all the "cold" and "bitter" talk—of the aesthetic time-tourist. He sees his "Phases", that is to say, as so many static "attitudes" and actor's "roles"—not as organically related. This is apt to be hidden by the continuous development of his expressive power, though it is significant that clumsiness in *transitions* remained, up to the last, his greatest—perhaps his only—technical defect. The author's feat of remaining young in spirit—which makes his voice such an individual one, and which it seems ungrateful to regret—really implies a lack of true growth, and a deliberate choice of adolescent crudity and bravado. Crazy Jane is not more real than Queen Maeve—they are the two halves of the Swan-and-Leda dichotomy, and Yeats could never really bring them together: the monstrous nuptials remained infertile, as in fact monstrous nuptials usually do. I do not mean to say that W. B. Y. will not "stand the test of Time", but he himself was too little in love with "the productions of Time"; like the goddess in his poem *The Grey Rock*, he was always crying "Why must the lasting love what passes?" His chosen world of Platonic Forms (or, as he significantly called them, *Masks*) remained a literary

[1] In fairness one should perhaps also quote the accurate line, "The green shadow of Ferrara wall".

man's world—even if he created a marvellous sort of
literature of his own; as in his courtship of Maud Gonne
one feels he was half in love with frustration, and the
"mask" was a little also of a screen. And yet there was
another possibility in Yeats, as we feel in reading his
exhilarating *Samhain* articles on the Irish dramatic
movement, in the beginning of the century—so ardent
and yet realistic, combative but without bitterness—
essays which might be prefaces from a more sensitive
Bernard Shaw. Something, it would seem, broke
W. B. Y.'s courage in two, like those thorn-trees over
Cummen strand, separating him like a withering branch
from the green tree of life—that tree which he looks back
to, with a Goethe-esque reminiscence, in *Among School-
children*. He said that he would "wither into the truth",
but it was a partial truth only that he attained. For my
part I cannot deplore his choice, which turned an
"Elizabethan" into a "Metaphysical"—a poetic dramatist into a sort of dramatic lyricist; but it may have
involved a certain real loss to the world. Some sharp
experience, as I think, took him and turned him inwards
upon himself; and I believe it was the occasion when
patriotic mobs howled down *The Playboy of the Western
World*.

Yeats faced the storm manfully; but he never really
recovered from that exhibition of mass-intolerance, in
the country to which he had given so much of his hope.
That he had gone far in his own tolerance for national
bigotries is clear from the Dramatic Notes, where he
strained even his style to a painful, and very charming,
simplicity; but those brawls against art aroused all the
bigot in himself. Actually of course Yeats was unreason-
able, like every impatient idealist, for—patriot though

he was—he did not know his countrymen; and a people still close enough to the peasants whom Synge portrayed —ruthlessly if with gusto—could scarcely be expected to relish the portrait. The colourful peasant speech, which delights the cultivated, had less novelty for ordinary Irishfolk, who saw merely the naked brutality of the life described; for the motive of the villagers in sheltering the outlaw is not represented as pity, or the over-riding duty of hospitality, but as a simple admiration for violence. Further, *The Playboy* is in fact a very subtle and disturbing piece of work. At first sight it seems a play about an actor-type—a trenchant satire on the Irish weakness for bravado (just as the word "playboy" is an Irishism). Only of course Synge, Cervantes-like, fell in love with his hero, and turned that Mayo public-house—as Shaw in *Blanco Posnet* seemed to turn the villainous Western log-courthouse—into a bitter symbol of the world. Be all that as it may, the *Playboy* demonstrations—and the even more regrettable bickerings, about the same time, over the Lane Bequest—did something to Yeats; they changed him, like an inverted St. Paul, from an apostle into a *frondeur*. After these things, no events in the real world could deeply stir him. Abandoning his efforts to educate the people through the Stage, he became content to see the world as a Stage, remaining himself a disgruntled, if half-envious, spectator—feeling even that it would be a fine thing to commit violence on the roads with the "Irregulars" (*Meditations in Time of Civil War*). Even his plays were henceforth to be written for drawing-rooms. Despairing of ever really bringing art and life together, he became an aesthete in his life (more so, essentially, than he had ever been in the '90s, in spite of his Senatorship) and gave a factitious air of realism to his art:

singing of 18th Century lords and louts, instead of Red
Branch Knights and the spiritual peasant. And between
these extremes the image of living man—or rather the
man of to-morrow whom every true poet celebrates—
was somehow "blotted out". When reality broke in on
him forcibly, like Christy Mahon's live and blustering
parent in *The Playboy*, Yeats shivered away from the
impact; he did not thenceforth "go romping through
a romancing life-time", but became (at heart) life-
estranged—a Milton by no means mute or inglorious
or un-Miltonic, but yet a village Milton only. He fled
like love, in that excessively Yeatsian last line of his
sonnet from Ronsard—and "hid his face amid a crowd
of stars".

Yeats has told us that if he had been given a month of
Antiquity and leave to spend it where he chose, he would
have spent it in Byzantium, a little before Justinian
opened St. Sophia and closed the Academy of Plato. He
says,

> I think I could find in some little wine-shop some
> philosophical worker in mosaic who could answer all
> my questions, the supernatural descending nearer to
> him than to Plotinus even, for the pride of his delicate
> skill would make what was an instrument of power to
> princes and clerics, a murderous madness in the mob,
> show as a lovely flexible presence like that of a perfect
> human body.

We have here, in a succinct statement, the three levels of
the philosophy at which Yeats arrived: the murderous
madness of the mob (associated to the "murderous innocence" of his "gong-tormented sea")—the *Realpolitik* of

princes and prelates—the "lovely flexible presence" of art, produced from these two as by shock and counter-shock, comparable perhaps to the rose-tree that grew out of the graves of the lovers Baile and Ailinn, or the divine Helen from the sporting of bird and woman. This illustrates perhaps the fault and the danger of Yeats's too-theatrical way of thought—a formalism reminding one slightly of Celto-Byzantine ornament, or the politics of Mr. De Valera! Such a scheme ignores—I do not say "progress"—but a certain undeniable evolution, for good and for bad, in human society: that developed ingenuity which has enlarged, on the one hand, the mob's powers of destruction, and, on the other, the spiritual complexity of individuals taken singly. It is at least possible today for the dialectic to be an inner one—for the individual to generate the spirit of art out of his own contradictions, instead of having to engage in frenzied political dramas: dramas which are more likely to obliterate art—and all human life—than to create any new and "terrible" beauty. Yeats might have been taught by the contemporary Irish story, which had so deeply affected him; but it was his tragedy that he passed from hatred of the "passionate intensity" of fanatics to a quasi-admiration for it. The murderous madness of 1922, the (consequent) increased power of governments and clerics—all this was possibly inevitable, but it has not (as so many of us once hoped it would) issued in an artistic rebirth. Its chief effect in that direction has been, indeed, to blight us with a Censorship.

Both Shaw and the later Yeats abounded in denunciations of the Mob—in its modern newsprint-fed semi-literate form. In this, indeed, they would have my heartiest sympathy, were it not that their dislike of the Mob was vitiated by ideas of Superman and of Class (princes and prelates indeed!): for every Class or Race is in fact but another mob—and Yeats knew it when he wrote the disillusioned little poem "Church and State".[1] The true and fundamental antithesis is between Mob and *Man*, between mere numbers and the free spirit. Democracy is the best and worst of doctrines—the best when it safeguards the rights of individuals and minorities, the worst when it exalts the Mass. The Greek name for mass-despotism is *ochlocracy*, and the modern one is *totalitarianism*: both words unfortunately are difficult to say, which has led to the issue being confused with questions (really secondary) of fascism, communism, etc. But it is true that the good democracy turns all-too-easily into the bad, if it be not stiffened with a framework of classes (just as poetry—Yeats insisted—turns to mush or propaganda if it be not stiffened with symbols). That is the real case for aristocracy, and not any supposed superiority of aristocrats—who, in fact, have usually been as uncultured and unreliable as their own horses. It is more sensible to regard the "upper classes" as a nuisance which had better be borne—because the alternative to them is a "blackguardocracy" of political arrivistes. A true democracy is a polity in which one is permitted to curse them—and, within defined limits, to tax them. As a Frenchman summed up the matter, it is a society in which one can say *merde*.

The anti-democracy of Yeats and Shaw was in fact the nostalgia of the mere "actor" and the literary man

[1] . . . That were a cowardly song,
Wander in dreams no more;
What if the Church and the State
Are the mob that howls at the door! . . .

for the life of Action—which both of them felt keenly: that life by which Yeats, when he tried to approach it, had been so rudely rebuffed. They saw themselves in their dreams as leaders—a fancy which comes (or came) easily in Ireland to the descendants of the colonists; and they forgot that the leader today must be either democrat or demagogue. In this matter, as we have seen, the anti-romantic Shaw was quite as romantic as the mythologist Yeats—even if he was more "altruistic". But he was also less pardonable, for international politics were his proper concern, whereas Yeats had no knowledge—and scarcely claimed any—of the politics of other nations than his own. Yeats, in spite of his desire to be a public figure, was more apolitical than any fully responsible person alive; even his impressive poem *The Second Coming* was suggested chiefly, it seems, by the Irish "troubles". "I am told there is a law in Germany" he remarked in 1935 "by which noblemen can be given back their hereditary castles"[1]—and that was all he knew about the obscene demagogy which priced Einstein's head like a criminal. Nor, I think, did he realise—or care to realise—the extent to which the less savoury elements of the magical tradition had contributed to that witch-broth. It is this insular simplicity which accounts, in part, for the slight air of patronage with which Yeats is still treated by the critics, as contrasted with the respect accorded to some—on the whole—lesser figures. "You were silly like us—your gift survived it all" wrote W. H. Auden, a little too perkily. If an anthology of impudence could be compiled from the dicta of Shaw, it would be as easy to put together a herbarium of naïveté from the remarks of Yeats—even if it was a wilful and not altogether serious

[1] I owe this quotation to Cecil Salkeld.

naïveté. Yeats was perhaps fortunate to die in 1938; for he seemed, like his friend Ezra Pound, to be doodling when Rome was burning—or rather, "like another Helen", to be lighting the way for the incendiaries.

At the same time I may be permitted to point out, as an Irishman, that Yeats was not only Irish by birth but an Irish patriot—an old disciple of the Fenian O'Leary, and even vaguely a member of the Irish Republican Brotherhood. There was no reason to demand of him a traditional respect, such as an Englishman very rightly feels, for the British Constitution. He had as much right to favour some form of authoritarianism as had any Italian or French bourgeois; the more so as it seemed doubtful, in the '20s and '30s, whether any rule but dictator-rule could succeed in the new Irish state. So far was he from being merely a "snob" that he once, out of respect for his revolutionary past, refused a title.[1] On the other hand, his brief flirtation with General O'Duffy's "blueshirts" was something of a pro-British peacemaking gesture; by one of the paradoxes of Irish politics, democracy was then represented by the separatist party of De Valera, whose government was at that time waging a senseless anti-British economic war. All this was forgotten in 1939, when it was remembered simply that Yeats—like many Englishmen with none of his excuses—had once had a few good words for the Dictators.

Yeats cannot without qualification be called a fascist; nor was he (in spite of his dubious Nietzschean theories concerning Tragedy) what is ordinarily meant by an "immoralist". His pamphlet *On the Boiler* contains this admirable statement, setting him apart from the simple admirers of "blood and instincts":

[1] Hone, *Life*, p. 311.

I detest the Renaissance because it made the human mind inorganic; I adore the Renaissance because it clarified form and created freedom. I too expect the Counter-Renaissance, but if we do not hold to freedom and to form it will come, not as an inspiration in the head, but as an obstruction in the bowels.

And in the same work he is moved to indignation by the sadism of Flecker's *Hassan*. Yeats could fall, when in his 18th Century vein, into tolerance of brutality; but his art is less streaked with cruelty even than that of Synge —who, like Flecker, was a sick man and a hunter of the exotic. Yeats's moral tone was always on the whole healthy and traditional, with something of the responsibility of a natural law-giver. As an "initiate" he was sternly opposed on moral grounds (some may be comforted to learn) to the sinister A. Crowley, and even on one occasion—it is said—deputed a vampire to plague him![1] For all that, Yeats was untouched—to an unexampled degree—by any conscious Christian influence: fortunately for him perhaps, since if he had been more of a Christian theist he might also have been more of a Satanist. With all his love of rituals and houses "famous for sanctity or architectural beauty", he never—that one knows—attended a religious service; the verse-theatre was his true church, as the concert-room (not, I should say, the theatre) was that of Shaw. He would seem to have regarded the Christian religion as a 5th Century Roman might have regarded it—simply as a more successful variant of Mithraism or the cult of Cybele. His plays *Calvary* and *The Resurrection*, without being at all blasphemous, would strike very strangely on a Christian

[1] The amusing story is told by R. Ellmann (*Kenyon Review*).

sensibility[1]—Jesus to him is a "god" but hardly God, and certainly not the Nazarene teacher. Though a mystic,[2] one wonders if he *really* read Baron von Hügel; and though a supernaturalist, it is doubtful whether he can be called a monotheist. The word "God" usually occurs in his writings with the vaguest of connotations; it means little more than that "irrational Force" which is constantly breaking in upon reason and settled order, like a shooting star or swooping bird—or like that cold "rook-delighting" light, whose effect on Yeats seems to have been a queerly hypnotic one. (In passing, it is interesting to note Yeats's fascination for objects which gleam or glitter: cats' eyes, jewels, herrings in a pile, rocks or waters with the sun on them, mirrors—and, of course, the metal bird.) "The stallion Eternity" sings Tom of Cruachan "mounted the mare of Time"; and

[1] In *Calvary*, Lazarus is represented as a philosophic pessimist who resents his resuscitation, the Roman soldiers as happy Pagans who have no desire to be saved, and Judas as an ironist who commits his treachery as a sort of *crime gratuit*. The tragedy of Jesus, it is suggested, is that these three "happy" types of men are beyond the need for the divine mercy; and this moral is reinforced by the musicians' refrain "God has not died for the white heron". A Christian would have shown the inadequacy of these various schools of thought when confronted with Reality. (Incidentally they represent, of course, Yeats's favourite trinity of "Saint", Fool and Hunchback—the three types of fatalism, in which he saw himself: and the third of these—the completely detached man—is always associated in Yeats's verse to the hump-backed heron. This gives a slightly sinister tinge to Yeats's apotheosis of the Actor. The most *dramatic* character in the world, one realises, is Judas: just as the period of the Second World War may be remembered as the Age of the Traitor.

[2] It is common to deny Yeats's right to be called a mystic—apparently because he was not an adherent of any recognised religion; just as it is denied that he was a philosopher, because he stood apart from modern schools of philosophy (though if Dr. Joad calls Shaw a Bergsonian Vitalist we have as much right to class Yeats as a neo-Hegelian). I understand a "mystic" to be anyone who seeks to pierce to the meaning of things through emotion or ecstasy, and a philosopher to be a man who makes the same attempt by way of speculative thought; and I would maintain that Yeats was one with the best minds in being something of both. Yeats once said that all great mystics—as distinct from mere pietists—have been great in intellect; and I believe the converse of this to be also true.

while I understand Yeats's thought, it is natural to contrast it with the conception of the Platonic or Christian mystic—that Eternity is crucified upon the rood of Time. The Creation he feels, in the Eastern manner, to have been the true and aboriginal "Fall": but, he adds gaily in one of his sexual songs,

> Where the crime's committed
> The crime can be forgot.

Yeats's world is in fact—quite instinctively and naturally —a pre-Christian one; his Second Coming is a Second Coming (at best) of Pan—not of Christ; his supernatural visitants are strangers or changelings—but little distinguished from those eternal *birds*—or they are ghosts, driven to wander by the injustice (not, be it observed, by the justice) of the "outrageous" skies. And it would seem that gods, birds and instinctive men are opposed in Yeats's thought to more conscience-burdened types: and that these—weighed to earth Prometheus-like by guilt and responsibility—wander disconsolately in the mazes of their past lives.

Whether Yeats "believed" in this farrago is less interesting, I think, than what he may have meant by it. This or something like it is the old belief of the world; though Yeats differs from the popular view in making repentance rather than crime itself the cause of hauntings. After all, the tenets of the orthodox Christian are to some minds no less astonishing. While he was as little a Christian as is possible for a religious person, Yeats—like so many introverts—was rather excessively tormented by conscience: though his perturbations, certainly, were not connected with sins, but rather with (another key-word in his writings) *responsibilities*. In his later poems he often sets a quasi-Jansenistic guilt-sense to dialogue against an antinomian self-will; he takes upon himself—exaggeratedly—responsibility for the Irish burnings, and, by extension, for the whole anarchy of the world and even "the crime of being born". This leads him to the paradoxical conclusion that we are "blest" by ridding ourselves of remorse—remorse that would blot out the brave past—that we do not obtain forgiveness by remorse, but forgive ourselves remorse's curse; though he would no doubt add the qualification that the Elect ("such as I") are, more than others, stricken with that curse. Repentance, he wrote, keeps my heart impure; but his hero Cuchulainn resists the seductions of the fairy-woman through "intricacies of blind remorse". The ever-returning horse-hooves in his fine play *Purgatory* are "impressions on my mother's mind"; it does not appear that the ignoble father either suffers or can forgive—nor has the mother committed any crime (beyond a little irresponsibility!) commensurate with her suffering.[1] And the play loses nothing even if we regard the ghostly hoof-beats as an old man's hallucination (due to remorse-pangs)—though Yeats no doubt meant more than this. The forgiveness, it would seem, consists in "following every action to its source"—in understanding that mutual implication of things which makes the total

---

[1] Yeats's theology leads him into some strange debates, worthy of St. Augustine —and in this we may remark his kinship to James Joyce. The old man in *Purgatory* whose mother's ghost appears in the window at each anniversary of the wedding-night, is tormented by the following speculation:

> But there's a problem: she must live
> Through everything in exact detail,
> Driven to it by remorse, and yet
> Can she renew the sexual act
> And find no pleasure in it, and if not,
> If pleasure and remorse must both be there
> Which is the greater?

Drama (in the case of the dead this is called "the Dreaming Back"): through it we unbind our particularity ("unpack the loaded pern"—"unwind the winding path") and become sinless like the birds—sinless but not indeed "spiritual"—rather, like Leda's Swan or the Virgin's Dove, engendering with a good conscience new cycles of generation and of ruin.

Such a doctrine (if I am right in thinking it was Yeats's) is certainly to be called "dangerous"; but it is after all logical, and partly sound, for one who is both an introvert and a lover of the world. Such a person must suffer by the world-tragedy morally—suffer by his sense of "involvement"—at the same time as he enjoys it aesthetically: he must clap his hands like a child at a play, even while he blames his enjoyment for being—in a sense—the final cause; and it is true there is no escaping this "double vision" so long as he is both an artist and a man. What is *not* true—what is indeed the fallacy of most Eastern mysticism, from the Bhagavad Gita downward—is the idea that the same person, at the same moment, can be both a perfectly dispassionate contemplator and a hot-blooded actor; to attempt this is to be a poor actor and certainly a partial, biassed, contemplator. (Curiously, Shaw's ironic superman-lovers exemplify the same fallacy in another way.) It is a well-known tendency, in the diverse Gnostic or Manichean cults, to pass from the inhumanly spiritual and refined to the sheerly earthy and orgiastic; and though this procedure can produce, in Art, the effect known as romantic irony, it is inadequate (to say the least) in Life—and in those forms of Art, such as the drama, which are deeply concerned with Life. That the "contemplator" can give us an aesthetic justification for cosmic evil—that the "actor" should have a certain Pagan glory in the person and presence—these are articles of Yeatsism (often foolishly called "fascist") with which no artist should quarrel; but for the contemplator to be a self-absolved actor or (in an older language) a "justified sinner"—at one and the same time Homer and the ravening raging Achilles— that is to try to make of the human being a kind of cen- taur or griffin, something impossible or monstrous. That Yeats never quite avoided this inhuman extreme is evident. Like his Magi, he tended to see in Christianity (and in the whole modern movement called liberalism) nothing but "turbulence"—the dominance of abstrac- tion and rhetoric; like his doll-maker, he was too apt to hearken to the dolls—the mythical monsters—and throw out the living baby. But he could also write, in *The Only Jealousy of Emer*, that "men are bound to women by the wrongs they do or suffer", and in *The Land of Heart's Desire*—although in this case Paganism wins the tussle— the moving lines,

<blockquote>

By love alone
God binds us to Himself and to the hearth,
That shuts us from the waste beyond His peace,
From maddening freedom and bewildering light.
</blockquote>

Those lines of the early Yeats have a devotional, almost Dantesque, sound. And yet, perhaps, they could not have been written by a Christian. Yeats's thought moves between this world of law and the other, amoral, world where is freedom and light[1]—the fantasy-world

---

[1] Yeats's two worlds, of course, continually melt and merge into each other— which gives his mind its peculiar scintillating quality (at times "bewildering" and "maddening" indeed) as of a bird's wing. Thus the "abstraction" of fanatics, which destroys the beauty he loves, seems itself the result of a bewitchment—as it were an arrow-shaft—from the world of cold transcendent beauty. Hence his

which is "the world's bane" (and the "brave delirium"
of Irish nationalism is not far from his mind); but God
has really nothing to do in the picture. Yeats enjoys his
"antinomies" too much to wish to "transcend" them;
although a typical modern case of split personality, he
does not suffer in the modern way from that condition.
On the contrary, he makes of it a real, if limited, artistic
effect[1]—just as, during his senatorship, he steered a
wary course between magnates and desperadoes. Though
it would be absurd to call him a "Calvinist", he exhibits
the very Calvinistic combination of determinism and
hypertrophy of the will—just as his attendant spirits
remind one a little (in Pagan dress) of those 17th Century
Protestant "motions of the spirit". Though he is continually called an "escapist" by younger critics, Yeats
lacks all pessimism or true world-weariness; he even
criticises the Catholicising tendency of his luckless *fin de
siècle* friends—on the rather surprising ground that it
deepened their despair and demoralisation (*Autobiographies*). Whether or no *The Shadowy Waters* was suggested by the Schopenhauerian *Axël*, its resemblance to
that philosophical drama is superficial, for the poem's
philosophy is as shadowy as its story. Like his early
teacher Morris, Yeats has something of the busy con-
tented child—Morris who was also an excellent man of
business and definitely "got things done". I have called
W. B. Y. a writer for minds that are solitary, but his
solitude was after all of the romantic sort; he was perhaps
too self-conscious, too fond of projecting himself into

recurrent theme of the decapitation or evisceration of the hero by "virgin cruelty".
Similarly the "desecration" of the Ideal by brute life completes the circle, and we
are back among the feathered race.

[1] This is shown nowhere more happily than in the subtle and charming song-
sequence of *The Lady and the Chambermaid*.

various roles, ever to be at the point where names and forms drop away—to know true solitude, or even intimacy.[1] His emotions are always very public ones— political anger, stoical defiance, love (of the so-called "Byronic" kind) for a celebrated beauty: not for him at any time the sorrows of a Dowson, silently pining for the café- keeper's daughter! Even his "holy dread" requires the séance or the circle of initiates. The Yeatsian hero "may know not what he knows, but knows not grief"—which, as von Hügel might have pointed out to him, is a senti- ment that knows nothing of the Cross. He speaks much, in the Nietzschean manner, of "tragic joy", without seeing the slight paradox in the concept; and in his *Oedipus at Colonus* he praises "a gay goodnight"—as a second-best to not-being—which is fine, but not Sophocles and scarcely (in the context) sense. "Man" he declares "has created death"; but in so far as this is true there cannot, clearly, be any tragedy, nor even the calm joy—the classic *catharsis*—of acceptance. His heroes

---

[1] Yeats is so protean a character that almost any statement one may make about him calls for instant qualification. In the long poem *Vacillation* he recounts the following incident (also recorded in prose in the volume *Per Amica Silentia Lunae*):

> My fiftieth year had come and gone,
> I sat, a solitary man,
> In a crowded London shop,
> An open book and empty cup
> On the marble table-top.
> While on the shop and street I gazed
> My body of a sudden blazed;
> And twenty minutes more or less
> It seemed, so great my happiness,
> That I was blessèd and could bless.

Whether or no this is properly to be called a mystical experience, it seems to me a very exact description of the ecstasy which is the occasional recompense of lone- liness. In these lines Yeats recalls a poet with whom he has, in general, slight affinity—namely Wordsworth.

and heroines cannot say, like Racine's *Phèdre*, "Soleil je viens te voir pour la dernière fois"; for they will see that bitter sun again many times, both in the spirit and in the flesh. Yeats has forgotten the fate of the Sorcerer's Apprentice—which, however, partly overtook him, and which supplies the only real notes of tragedy in his work. With Yeats, the supernatural world is a dressing-room, where the players change their masks or make-up between "incarnations"—a story-book *Hinterland* that gives a false depth to the real world, but with not much suggestion of a Buddhistic "liberation". He seldom feels Death, in the fashion of Rilke or of Lawrence (or, as we shall see, of Joyce), as the great Mystery and Unifier—a thing almost to be desired.[1] Supernatural terror he knew, but he had no longing for the Unknown. His nostalgia was not for death but for life; he was even like a man who had already died.

Yeats's great pageant of maskers in *A Vision* tails off in

---

[1] Against this may be quoted the last lines of *The Wheel*—

> Nor know that what disturbs our blood
> Is but its longing for the tomb.

But for Yeats (apart from the fact that we must not look in him for complete consistency) the word *tomb*, I think, is always used concretely—never merely as a metaphor; it is related to his (later) preoccupation with stone, bone, and all hard, bare, essential things. (T. M. Henn shows in his fascinating book how much Yeats responded to the marble-like art, and the intensity, of Mantegna.) That preoccupation, moreover, is not without a touch of the macabre, as in much modern verse. If the immortality of the ghost is Purgatory (because temporary), the immortality of the bone is Hell (because eternal). In *A Stick of Incense*, Yeats assimilates the "Virgin womb" to the "empty tomb", from which—as he conceives it—proceeded the religion of abstraction and death. The remainder of the poem is a (not very fortunate) paraphrase of "Where the crime's committed the crime can be forgot"; and the opposition between the *plenum* and the *vacuum* is given a further sinister twist in the two stanzas *Oil and Blood*. "Too long a sacrifice can make a stone of the heart"—and conversely, the stone is hungry for sacrifice. It seems strange that Yeats nowhere (to my knowledge) makes use of Plato's Cavern—that image under which abstract reason first "emptied the gnoméd mine".

a triad that has become famous—the three thin emana-
tions, as he conceived them, of the waning Crescent of
our era: the Hunchback, the Saint and the Fool. The
Fool has a long history as the first and last card of the
Tarot pack—the Joker of our ordinary playing-cards.
Where Yeats got his Hunchback and his Saint from I
cannot discover—unless it was indeed from those ghostly
"Instructors": for the Saint is not, clearly, the Christian
Saint, but one who "has renounced even the desire for
his own salvation"—he comes at the instant when
synthesis (even the false synthesis of utopian socialism)
is abandoned, when fate is accepted. But the twain may
stand very well for two typical figures of the age: the
pure extravert and the pure introvert, the "Commissar"
and the "Yogi", the mechanistic man who lacks tradition
and the spiritual man who lacks integration. And the
Fool is he who lacking all, being empty both of faith and
will—passive both in resistance and acquiescence—may
be the vessel of new life; he is the Simpleton in the Fairy
Tales who wins in the end—the *je-m'en-foutiste* who tosses
up at every crossroad—that pathetic-ironic character
who is the true hero of the most modern books and plays.
In the world of Yeats, and in his alone, he still has his
cap and bells—for the clowns of Rilke and Picasso are
mirthless; but that is because with Yeats he is still a
court-fool, with his niche in a solemn hierarchy. Yeats
approximates most clearly to the type of the Saint—if I
have understood his description of that personage; but
he fades at the edges, so to speak, into Hunchback and
Fool. The "Hunchback" is represented by Bernard
Shaw—the Caesar-worshipper, the lamed artist and first
of the journalists; the Fool is James Joyce, the creator
of Leopold Bloom—Jewish commercial traveller and

cuckold. These three puppet-makers, as I see them, are themselves the puppets in the soul's-comedy of today.[1]

. . . . .

And yet Yeats's influence has been, by comparison with that of his rivals, very small; and, except by students of poetic technique, he is little studied. For with all his industry and practical energy—his view of himself as the laureated official bard—one is continually struck by his strangeness. Truly he was not of earth (like Keats) or heaven (like Shelley) nor again of hell (like Byron and the *poètes maudits* of Bohemia). His true country was what he called "Purgatory"—a world of phantoms (like the Christ in *The Resurrection*) in whom the heart nevertheless beats—a world of piercing light, "gyring" birds and naked trees[2]—a Russian-ballet universe of frozen energy and "agonies of flame that cannot singe a sleeve": a world which yet is a true reflex of the *emptiness* and the peculiarly electric air of Ireland. His verse, as he grew older, did not really become more human, but only more effectively histrionic; the mask fitted better and came to look more like a face. The very Joycean "Thoth, god of writers, birdgod, moony-crowned": or one might compare him to the Unicorn of his *Player Queen*, that was vulnerable to nothing but a spear dipped in the blood of a dragon which had died

[1] If anyone should protest that I am stretching Yeats's categories unduly, I shall be content to say (what I think will be granted) that Hunchback, Saint and Fool are the three constituent parts of every Irishman; and every country (but Ireland perhaps particularly so, because of her isolation) is a microcosm of the world.

[2] An unsympathetic critic might compare it rather to the Grove of the Harpies in the *Inferno*—those human-faced birds which *fanno lamenti in su gli alberi strani*. Yeats's birds, be it observed, do not sing: at best they shriek. They have never the lyric, pathetic, significance of (for example) the nightingales in the verse of T. S. Eliot.

gazing on an emerald—for only by such complicated strategy could reality reach him. Chesterton objected that Yeats did not understand Faery-land, because the fairy-tales always teach the lesson of obedience; he failed to notice that the fairies, like the natural forces which they typify, *dictate* a course of action to those who would deal with them—they do not themselves *obey*, but merely act according to their natures. But the truth is that Yeats was far too little of a Christian, or even of a well-trained human being, to please Chesterton. There will always be those who will look on him, slightingly, as an aesthete—one who simply lived longer than the other aesthetes; but the fact that he survived the "Nineties", and lifted aestheticism with infinite pains into great art, shows that the *fin de siècle* was also a *commencement de siècle*—that the late fruiting held one good seed for the age to come. For the time has arrived for the artist to resolve the antinomies of religion and science, to assume in his turn the burdens of philosopher and guide—in a world which no longer listens to the priest, and has begun to view the scientist with despondency and even alarm: to bring back old gods—without romanticising them as "dark" like Lawrence, nor even as shining, in the excessive Yeatsian way. Certainly no poet ever created so much good poetry out of so exiguous materials—he seemed to build an art out of his rejections till his verses were nothing but light and outline; but the fact makes him perhaps something more than a poet—a philosopher of an almost forgotten kind, of a time when truth and beauty grew from the same stem, and were known by the now remote-sounding name of "wisdom". Yeats's inhumanity puzzles, repels, and a little frightens: but it frightens us into a sort of metaphysical awareness, like that of a citizen of the "other world" who returns to tell us its secrets. His mummy-wheat is more wholesome than the breakfast-cereals of the college-"courses"; and I think of him supping at journey's end with Hegel and Heraclitus, as well as with Landor and with Donne.

We have seen that Yeats's "joyful tragedy" is a paradox that has a tendency to neutralise itself.[1] Its result—in *A Full Moon in March*—is something dangerously close to sadism: only Yeats, though he might fringe on satanism and sadism, was preserved from both by what Peter Allt has called his fineness of "instinctive moral taste". And equally his *Minnesingerdienst* to the amazonian Maud Gonne was too much like a delicious masochism for us to take him quite tragically. But this is not to say that there is no element of tragedy in his life and work. The idealist philosophy of Germany—just because it is, so to speak, *pure* philosophy—slips all-too-easily into solipsism, from which so many entanglements of nations are seen to grow; and Yeats—who read extreme idealism into Berkeley, and hated realism in thought as in art[2]—was not free from this danger.

[1] "Tragic joy"—or, more simply, the habit of treating tragedies as farces—is a rather typically Irish attitude. Bernard Shaw, who was himself inclined to this sort of perversity, expressed a sensitive revulsion from it through the mouth of Peter Keegan: "It *is* hell. Nowhere else would such a scene be a burst of happiness for the people". But Shaw and Yeats seem to agree (for once!) in liking nothing of Shakespeare but the Elizabethan swagger and Machiavellism.

[2] In some ways Yeats is closer to "realism" (in the modern sense) than to the classical "idealism": with him it is the Dream, so to say, that is real—the Subject is passive Dreamer rather than active Thinker. His interest in spirits is foreign to idealist thought; he abuses F. H. Bradley for not desiring "survival", but he could have found the same fault in his Italian neo-Hegelians. Yeats welcomes the modern theories of flux (with the correction that "the flux is in my own mind") and he traces the decline of English poetry since the 17th Century to the sway of materialist physics. "Europe" he wrote to a friend in 1933 "belongs to Dante and the witches' cavern, not to Newton". Materialism, however, has had many poets, from Lucretius to Fitzgerald: it preserves at least the religious notion of Eternal Law, and the subsistence and shapes of Objects. If it cannot produce a Dante, neither does it boil down poetry in a "vitalist" witches' cavern.

("Whatever flames upon the night/Man's own resinous heart has fed.") Neither "moral taste" nor "holy dread" are the same thing as reverent awe: and reverent awe is impossible to the solipsist, as it is completely lacking in the poetry of Yeats. His declared ideal was "to live for contemplation and yet keep our intensity": and that, we have seen, is a have-it-both-ways aim, which is apt to mean contemplating one's own emotions only. Just as the man who tries to make himself God becomes devilish, so the man who would be "a god" tends to become, as it were, a ghost—something unreal. Yeats's attitudes really resolve themselves into two—bravura and terror— according to whether the "bird-" or human part of him is uppermost; and the terror has certainly nothing of joy. To regard existence, survival and rebirth merely as tragedy, and yet to desire them, is nothing but a stoical flourish—an attitude impossible to sustain; his early play *Deirdre*, which powerfully conveys terror, is partly falsi-fied by the self-conscious histrionics of the protagonists (". . . naught's lacking/But a good end to the long, cloudy day"). W. B. Y.'s famous epitaph[1] seems like the usual 18th-Centuryism, till one realises—almost with a shock—that he is apostrophising his own shade! He him-self is the cold horseman who must for ever ride—because Life and Death have passed him by. Everyone must feel that his plays about ghosts—*The Dreaming of the Bones*, *The Words upon the Window-pane*, *Purgatory*—are more real and human than his plays about the living: these people have found no comfort in the grave because their creator attained no true happiness in the body. In *The Words upon the Window-pane* Yeats has in fact utilised the séance

[1] Cast a cold eye
On life, on death.
Horseman, pass by!

to good artistic purpose—it is the only modern thing which he has so used! We get the same thrill as from Shakespeare's play-within-the-play in *Hamlet*, which catches the conscience of the king. But we realise that for Yeats the tragic figure is really Claudius, doomed for ever to pour poison into a sleeping ear,—bound to a meaningless and hateful ritual—, and not the Prince of Denmark.

Yeats's nearest affinity is perhaps with another poet-dramatist, Goethe: Goethe who also, to a certain degree, turned a split personality into a source of strength—who was also in contact with pre-Christian myth and the hermetic tradition—who also took a pride, part civic and part snobbish, in public functions and dignities—who in the same way combined physical stamina and besetting ill-health. Both Yeats and Goethe at all times took themselves with a seriousness which at first repels, but gradually forces our admiration; both developed slowly from sorrowing Werthers into wise but rather wild old men—and Yeats's *Autobiographies* are not a little reminiscent, by their style, of *Dichtung und Wahrheit*. But . . . while Goethe can be compared to a massive German *Schloss*, Yeats is more like the refurbished Ballylee Tower ("half dead at the top", as he mournfully remarked). Goethe stands four-square in the centre of his age and in the centre of the agitated world: while Yeats was always, for good and ill, a little outside of time and space. Yeats should have been, and had dreamed of being, the flower and crown of his nation in its greatest century—as Dante was of Italy, Shakespeare of England, Racine of France, Goethe of Germany. This he failed to be: partly because the time of homogeneous nations is gone, partly because he was too little interested in ordinary people to be a popular dramatist—even if a drama both popular and poetic were possible today. His *Cathleen ni Houlihan* crystallised the national dream for one burning moment, but the moment quickly passed; his poems on the Easter Rising—magnificent though they are—seemed to his countrymen aloof and patronising, like unasked-for "official poems" from a self-appointed laureate. Irish nationality was born both too late and too early for literary purposes: too late because the nation had really lost its symbol, the language—too early because in Ireland nationality and the medieval church are still one indivisible concept. Ireland missed the Renaissance, and Yeats—though doubtfully of the Reformation—was certainly of the Renaissance; and— for as much as that mattered—he had not the Gaelic. He and the movement he started are still looked at askance in Eire, as Pagan—even foreign—things: Coole Park, their symbol and shrine, was pulled down following its sale by a Government Department, without arousing the smallest protest. He dreamed of bringing together the heroic legends and the folklore tradition; but the first never really entered into modern Irish life and thought, and the second was a tradition that Ireland—both for religious and understandable mundane reasons—was only too anxious to turn her back on. Once again Yeats was seeking an impossible conjunction: his ideal, to think like a wise man and speak like the "common people" of his country, an ideal quite admirable in theory, could only be achieved today at the cost of much strain and artificiality—by falling back on that literary character, the inspired Village Idiot. The new Ireland did not see itself in Crazy Jane and Tom the Lunatic; and it had few tender memories of the class to which Yeats was, pardonably, proud to belong—the Anglo-Irish.[1] To his Catholic countrymen Anglo-Ireland did not mean Swift, Berkeley, Burke and Goldsmith, but Castle Rackrent and Beresford's "Riding School" and the murderer of the Colleen Bawn. In short, the Irish Leda would have none of the Swan. There were to be burnings enough: but no second Troy, no Irish Homer.

And yet Yeats is probably the last—the very "singing swan"—of that great Succession in which Homer is the first: poets for the ear more than the eye (generally nowadays the spectacled eye)—poets for whom mood and idea were still simple enough always to have a concrete visual equivalent. Yeats already is not quite simple, and in him the visual equivalents have shrunk, almost, to a bag of toys: there is a sense of something a little wire-drawn and creaking—for after all, it is no real swan that sings! After him the ladder and stage are taken down— we are left with nothing but "the foul rag-and-bone shop of the heart", or, as it is now called, the Unconscious; and out of it a totally new poetry will doubtless arise—is already arising—a poetry less personal, less national, less (in the old sense) religious,—a poetry whose first avatar was the ironic prose-Homer, James Joyce. Technically it will have learned something from the later Yeats, intellectually it may yet condescend to learn from him, but its spirit—for good and ill—will not be his. It will not be proud, passionate, intense, cold, and the rest of it; for we have seen what these attributes mean when translated into life under modern conditions—there is indeed no longer health in them. A romantic attitude consciously maintained against nature and historic logic

1 "Anglo-Irish" was not however a term that had any place in Yeats's vocabulary, any more than it had in that of the 18th Century Protestant Irish whom he admired.

turns always to something ugly—a truth which Bernard Shaw, in his comic Inferno, *almost* perceived: magic becomes black magic. It was Yeats's isolation that kept his romanticism comparatively sweet, and that preserved him from the modern irrationalism: he had not heard of what Peter Drucker has called "the Return of the Demons"—or he conceived it over-picturesquely and falsely. His "demons" (those of *The Countess Cathleen* and *The Two Trees*) were the Darwinians and agnostics of his youth—or else they were the joke-demons of the séance—and in this respect he remained to the end a Victorian. He said that what poetry stood in need of was the Vision of Evil, but by evil he meant merely earthiness, for Yeats had no realistic sense of evil.[1] Nevertheless, W. B. Y. was no "library-poet"—he assimilated, at each stage of his life, as much of modernity as his elaborately-fashioned "system" could digest. It is significant that he saw Cathleen ni Houlihan (a dreary conventional figment for most Irishmen) in a vivid living young beauty who will be remembered beside Dante's Beatrice and Petrarch's Laura—as well as being a good deal more interesting than either of them: almost as if Joan's Gilles de Rais had been a singer and not a sadist. And that his romance —here at least—was more than a conscious romanticism is proved by the rare tenderness of such lyrics as *The Pity of Love* and *The Folly of Being Comforted*. Nor did Yeats ever for a moment cease to develop as a poet, even if it was at the cost of his development as a man. For the normal development of a man today is, inevitably, away from poetry: there is so much new material to be

---

[1] Yeats criticised Shelley (in *Autobiographies*) for lacking the Vision of Evil—a surprising criticism if one remembers *The Cenci*. One hardly dares to imagine how Yeats would have handled the same theme—with what aristocratic virtues he would have endowed the hoary reprobate.

dealt with, which—for the moment—the novel and the prose-play seem alone able to contain. Yeats's line of growth, though apart from his age, was almost unswervingly parallel with it: so that he gives us, so to say, the complete life-cycle of subjective man in our time—the Other Self who is in all of us—the anti-cycle to our objectivity. For in every true democrat there is hidden an aristocrat, who at his moments is set free, like a ghost when the clock strikes twelve. He gives it moreover in words haunting and splendid, that charm while they challenge—so that he exacts from us an equal virtue if we would react against him. One could spend one's life in reading Yeats—it is indeed a temptation which I am constantly having to resist! But fortunately he stimulates by his thought as much as he delights by his form. And if the early Yeats delights more than he stimulates, it is at that age when youth, if it will look back to him, needs sedatives—stands more in need of the Yeatsian graciousness than of the Yeatsian passion. It may be disputed whether he wrote any poems as good as the best of some other men; I do not see how it can be disputed that he wrote lyrics which are good in a larger variety of modes, covering a greater stretch of moods, than any poet of our language. He could write political verse which yet was never turgid, social verse which was not merely trifling, philosophic verse which was not "meant to improve", bawdy verse which was not vulgar. One of his very first poems—*Who Will go Drive with Fergus Now?*— is a perfect poem: I thought so when I was as young as Yeats was when he wrote it, and I have not since gone back on my opinion. Almost his last poem—*The Circus Animals' Desertion*—is a great poem: I think so today, and I am certain that I shall think so no less (at least) when I am as old as Yeats was when he wrote it—if I live so long. It needs almost an effort to remember that the greatest writer of pure poetry since Milton (as he has been called) could also write lines like these, which might be sung by working men, and yet are poetry—

> The Bishops and the Party
> That tragic story made,
> A husband that had sold his wife
> And after that betrayed;
> But stories that live longest
> Are sung above the glass,
> And Parnell loved his country,
> And Parnell loved his lass.

     . .   . , ...

I do not believe all that Yeats believed, but there is a sense in which he gained in death the "Unity of Being" that he sought in life—the Sartrian sense that death gives life its form, its completion, and therefore its essence. Life is a continual *Becoming*, but to die is to enter into the immortality of the *Become*—to be fixed in the total picture like a mosaic in a wall. It is death that *judges* every life, giving to it its unalterable place in "the artifice of Eternity"—so that the hoof-beats of the drunken rider will for ever resound up the avenue, and the love-blinded bride for ever wait at the window— Hector trails in the mire and there's a light in Troy. In this sense, Yeats was one who living chose the dying world for text; without either loving the earth or longing for heaven, he saw all things standing, here and now, in the holy fire. By attaining to uttermost self-realisation in song, Yeats—beyond any man in our fevered age—

lived out his Purgatory and achieved the "breathless" state of Death in Life: the paradise of the artefact, the glory of changeless metal—*aere perennius*. By toying with mere Action as a "mask", he taught to practical men the unimportance of Action, and to philosophers its importance. He all but succeeded where the movement of the '90s failed, in justifying life and human history aesthetically, as the alternation and juxtaposition of moods—of all the notes in the psychical scale. That movement, which was art's "Declaration of Independence", was—like the Irish Easter Rising—a preliminary, rather sensational, flourish; it may be that a saner, more realistic, generation of philosopher-artists may carry it on to completion, and that Yeats will be seen as the De Valera who links the two. The aesthetic view of life, which holds more promise today than the religious or the scientific *Anschauungen*, has—like them—its fanatics and martyrs: of these Yeats—who from his Irish boyhood carried "a fanatic heart"—had something of the faults but more of the fineness. He made a faith out of an old jest—a philosophy to which the nominalism of the modern schools seems slowly to be groping its ponderous way: the claim that he made in youth and came near to vindicating in old age, that "words alone are certain good".

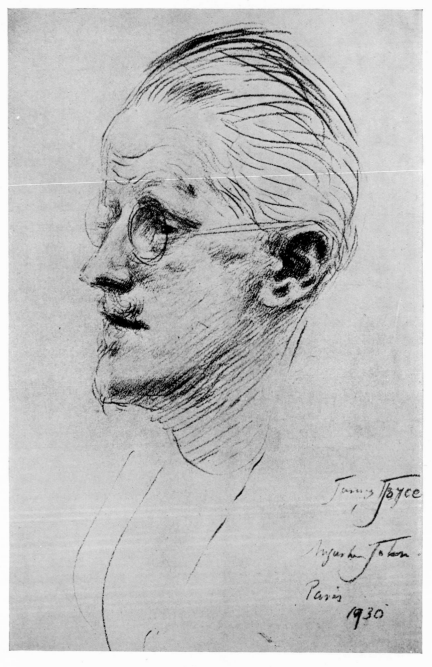

JAMES JOYCE

Drawing by Augustus John

III

James Joyce:

DOUBTING THOMIST AND JOKING JESUIT

A SPIRITUALIST SYMPOSIUM on *Finnegans Wake*.

Bernard-Shaw *dixit*:

When in the few moments that I relax from doing serious constructive work for the Fabian Society I consider the productions which take up socially-valuable space on the tables of drawing-rooms in our tea-besotted capitalist society, I can only regret that Lenin and Stalin did not give me the job of Head Commissar of the G. P. U., that I might liquidate the whole of that semiliterate morally-idiotic superfluous crew known as "intellectuals". The vicious doodlings of poetasters on the Liffey and the Seine may be of interest to vivisectionists, West End divas, and (possibly) themselves, but the whole literary output of capitalist countries since Ibsen (with the exception of my prefaces, plays and books) could be turned into pulp for stuffing communist mattresses without a single honest working man being a penny the worse. The conviction has grown on me with my growth that the pathological condition known as the "literary temperament" is a by-product of idleness, a chronic inability to lead a decent useful life, a failure to master the perfectly unanswerable analyses of capitalism by Karl Marx and myself, and (I suspect) an incapacity to read, spell, or understand a simple exposition of the rules of grammar. I thank the Life Force that prevented me wasting my unrivalled intellect among nasty-minded egoists in Dublin, and sent me by the first ship in which I could scrape up the fare to travel steerage to a country where people think cleanly and act sanely—or will do when we have sold a few more thousand copies of the Webbs' book on Soviet Russia.

G. K. Chesterton *dixit*:

What the modern world will never understand is that the only way to be modern is to be unmodern. The medievals believed in insanity—and therefore they tried hard to be sane. The ethereal energy of Gothic spires, the luminous logic of Aquinas, the mighty and masculine synthesis of Dante, the spontaneous organisation of guilds and crusades, were all so many express-trains to one terminus—the happier and higher lunacy. But the modern world starts in Bedlam and stays there; when it tries to shake the laws of logic and the commandments of Christian morality it can only rattle its bars—like that eminent Jewish financier I——during his late involuntary retirement. The modern man believes on the authority of myth-makers called scientists the (utterly unproved) dogmas that one is born, grows old and finally dies, and therefore he reacts into the puling half-wittedness of infantility; medieval man knew by the free use of his reason that it would be truer to say people are first old and progress continually towards the nursery, and therefore his spirit grew strong and mature as the beer and cider in the cellar of an old English inn. The era which thought it had advanced beyond "Mariolatry" has come full-circle and invented what it horribly calls a "Mother-Complex"; the age which laughed at Hell has rediscovered it, and renamed it "the Jungle of the Subconscious" —for Hell it has substituted Hanwell. The modern sage

who followed the star rising in the Protestant North has
come through barren places, by strange and twisted
roads to another Bethlehem, but the lowings of friendly
oxen are changed to gibbers and shrieks, and the Holy
Child in the crib is pickled in methylated.

W. B. Yeats *dixit*:

Beauty comes to us as a lady of the late 16th Century,
or late 17th Century—before thought had grown positive
and argumentative—wearing her domino and chastising
her negro page with a thin wand of white ivory. Swans
and peacocks flutter around her hair or sit on her
shoulders, and no sound is heard in her precincts before
midnight, when the vampires creep out of the tombs in
the chapel, and the shadows of elementals flit among
the over-hanging grapes in the courtyard, and wine-
drenched sounds of kisses float up through her windows
from the brothels in the harbour. The brawlers in the
market-place of Realism must stand aside when she
passes, and the orange-sellers of Psychological Fiction
must wipe the garlic from their lips before they kiss her
slipper. Our literature has forgotten the Mask, and like
a plain serving-wench any scullion can tickle her to
make her grin and wriggle. Hobson and Jobson, friends
of my youth, long since dead or crippled from their dis-
solute living, used to shut themselves up for hours in a
dark cupboard, slightly redolent of the products of the
dairy and the byre, having convinced themselves that
the Absolute could only be caught, like a mouse in a
springe, by a mind which had blotted out every image
of bird or fish or woman—in fact every image whatsoever. The experiment was, I believe, a failure; but I was
reminded of that brave delirium when I read the other

day a poem (or it may have been a work of fiction) sent to me by a friend who lives above an old wine-shop in the neighbourhood of Notre-Dame. He is old, and his life has been passed among symbols.

Mr. Sidney Carton of "The Citizen" *dixit*:

Mr. Joyce is a young man whose career we shall watch with interest, and we congratulate him on a brilliant first book. He represents the generation which grew up under the depression created by the folly of our Blimps and Tories, with its train of miseries leading from the deflation inaugurated by the owlishly-insane Report of the Cunliffe Committee, through a world-wide slump, to the growth of Fascism, and finally the Second World War. Under these circumstances we should not expect to find balanced thought or ordered expression in this book; nor do we find it. This book is in fact the most crushing indictment of the stupidity of the Old Men of Munich that could be imagined. Mr. Joyce is clearly a young man of considerable talents, who has been forced into the role of a bitter and destructive critic of this whole "sorry scheme of things". If we might offer a word of criticism which is meant to guide and not to disparage, we would suggest that in his next book he gives us more of the explanatory footnotes which appear, and then puzzlingly disappear, about midway through the work— without, unfortunately, throwing more than the fitfullest ray of clarification on the adjacent text. A little tightening up, a little teasing to take the lumps out of the mattress, a little thinning of the soup as it were, and we should have here a very valuable psychological study of a passing (we hope, already past) state of society.

. . . . .

JAMES JOYCE

The first fact to be realised about James Joyce (which the more earnest Joyceans seem strangely to overlook) is that he is a great humorous writer. A humorist who claims, or is claimed, to be great (or, in other words, to be something more than a humorist) causes always two-fold embarrassment: firstly among grave men, who could otherwise ignore him, and secondly among the *mere* jokers—like so many of Joyce's countrymen. It is, I fear, true that Catholic Ireland, by and large, has not yet heard of her greatest son—or heard of him only as a squalid expatriate, who wrote some blackguardly books in Paris, calling for immediate suppression by the authorities. But there is also an ingenious school which believes that Joyce dedicated his industrious life to the —doubtless delightful—task of hoaxing the public: much as the constructors of the Round Towers have been asserted to have had no other object in view than that of puzzling posterity.

Those who argue thus are perhaps too crude to be worth answering seriously; nevertheless, one can sympathise with them more than with that earnest sect for whom the world began on June 16th 1904 in the Holles St. Hospital. As Jeremiah, according to Voltaire, passed his life in weeping because a certain Leblanc would one day translate him, so Joyce must have derived some quiet mirth from the prevision of all those Harvard theses. And Joyce's humour was of the quiet—even sly— variety; the revelation of each of his quirks was as carefully planned as the explosion of a time-bomb. Even the pattern of *Ulysses* was made known, after a due interval, through Valéry Larbaud—like a sensation-"story" which a statesman releases by a hint to the press.

The world would have lost little, it always seems to me,

if the secret had not been divulged, or if the reader had been permitted to discover his own analogies: for the chief qualities of *Ulysses* are the un-Homeric ones of urbanism and urbanity. *Ulysses* is the great book of the town—the modern epic of Everyman: the better title for it would have been *Bloomsday*. The town is a modern capital, but one small enough for the protagonists' paths continually to cross. The central figure is the modern homeless man of the towns—the first, almost, of the "little men" of contemporary literature, and not the least appealing: the quintessential *petit bourgeois*—information-crammed, benevolent, hedonistic, pathetic. (Significantly, we never hear of a co-relative "little woman" —the modern townswoman, the Marion Bloom, seems always a shade nearer to the mythical origins than the man; and Molly is, rightly perhaps, a more "monstrous" creation than Leopold.) Leopold Bloom is a type—and he is also one of the great characters; though he is in some details out of date (as in his parochialism that has not even seen foreign warfare), we recognise him more easily today than when he was first created. He is a little also, of course, a burlesque—but not, it seems to me, an altogether apt one of the adventurous and cunning Odysseus. His true ancestor is another, far different Greek—who indeed but Socrates, the first of the rationalists and argufiers, Socrates of the difficult spouse and the poet-protégé. It is of the Platonic Socrates I think while I read that endless Bloom-Dedalus meditation, broken only by Thrasymachus-Citizens and Alcibiades-Mulligans; as I see in Joyce himself a hyperborean incarnation of Plato—he who turned his back on verse-writing to create philosophic biography.

The Homeric burlesque, I repeat, seems to me a little

over-strained, as it is the cause of some superfluous obscurity in Joyce's epic of a Clock-Round (for instance, in the "overture" to the musical Sirens-episode—a first anticipation of his later debauches of onomatopoeia). Circe may pass for the brothel scene, and Hades for that of the funeral; but we scarcely think of Scylla and Charybdis when reading the disputation in the Library, or of the Oxen of the Sun in connection with the Maternity Hospital. Yet if Joyce had coupled the midwifery-chapter with the Meno and the Library with the Republic, the lupanar-visit with the Symposium[1] and the funeral with the Phaedo—if he had done this the work would have gained in point without losing anything of its wit, and without requiring any very laborious exegesis. Joyce, in the eighteen episodes of *Ulysses*, found a handy framework for diurnal and nocturnal experience, as Yeats in the twenty-eight Moon-Phases (which have also their analogue in the twenty-eight schoolmisses of *Finnegans Wake*) found a natural setting for human types; for both the two Celts—obsessed, like John Scotus, with circles—had caught a Vesuvian spark from the proto-Hegelian Neapolitan, Vico. And Joyce, one imagines, hit upon the Odyssey for no other reason than because his own life was an Odyssey (perhaps also as a reaction and "carry-on" from the "Helen of Troy" heroic bardry of Yeats). The life of Mr. Bloom, however, could hardly be described as an Odyssey ("except you call going to Holyhead which was his longest")—any more than could that of the youthful Stephen Dedalus; though they had a good deal of an Athenian *peripatos*. Indeed the only really Odyssean character in the book is

[1] Or, even better, with the traditional scene in which Plato—having summoned his friends to a banquet—announces his abandonment of poetry in order to follow Socrates, and in token of his resolution heaps all his manuscripts on the fire.

the talkative sailor in the cabman's night-shelter. Actually, although many styles are parodied in *Ulysses* (including that of the Gaelic sagas) there are none of those parodies of Homer, common in novels of the picaresque tradition; and a Homeric student might read the book from end to end without being conscious of the adaptation—an adaptation to which Joyce, as we know, devoted the minutest care.

However *Ulysses*, of course, is something more than a mock-epic; and it is likely that more readers have been puzzled by the seeming irrelevance of its title than wearied by that—at times—laboured analogy. It is neither, altogether, a satire upon the present nor a burlesque of the past, but a serio-comic bringing-together of the two—a new and intensely interesting kind of symbolist epic, a more ebullient achievement in the *genre* of Mr. Eliot's *Waste Land*. For the Scholastically-taught Joyce, philosophy meant Aristotle, while the imaginative life meant the Odyssey—transmitted in school through the pleasant, if slightly pedestrian, re-telling of Charles Lamb; and the contrast of Aristotle and Homer gave him perhaps the peculiar tension—between prose and poetry, theory and myth, the "unities" and universality, time and eternity—which produced *Ulysses*. Only an author who was Irish by birth, but Catholic-continental by culture, could have cooked the Flaubertian *tranche de vie* over these two furnaces—could have made of realism (to paraphrase a famous saying) something solid and enduring like the literature of the schools. *Ulysses* is not only a great comic book but a great comedy—in the sense that Dante's vision was so named: a total reflex of existence, in which all tensions are resolved. It is significant that the young Joyce had written in his note-book,

"Tragedy is the imperfect manner and comedy the perfect manner in art". There is tragedy in *Ulysses* in the sense that modern man is most keenly aware of tragedy —that of the isolation of the soul; but there is also the consciousness, ironic yet exuberant, of the "ineluctable" community of the flesh. Marion Bloom—recumbent on her bed—is the still point round which the whole machine turns: the place where parallels meet and contraries coincide. She is not an actor, but she is the Primum Mobile of this Joycean cosmos, by Aristotle out of Bergson. Life is a tangle of masculine aspirations and cross-purposes, but her interior monologue (it is felt) goes on for ever.

The analogy with Dante is certainly no deeper than the one with Homer, though Joyce himself—another outcast (as he saw himself) from his native city—seems to have given it welcome. It is to be hoped the commentators do not get to work on it seriously, or we shall soon have Molly Bloom presented to us as Beatrice—just as the brothel-chapter (bracketed, in the Homeric scheme, not with "Hades" but with "Circe") has often been described as an *Inferno*.[1] Joyce was as little of a romantic

[1] I am aware that, according to some of Joyce's intimates who knew his mind well, *Ulysses* as a whole is to be regarded as his *Inferno*, *Finnegan* as his *Purgatorio*— because the language is "transitional" (and in fact the work first appeared in *transition*!); and we are even given to understand that the Master, before his death, had already written the sketch of a *Paradiso*. If Joyce really projected a work of the kind, I cannot help feeling that he was ill-inspired—seduced by his demon of pedantic schematism. All his work, it seems to me, may fitly be called "transitional" —and not only in the dubious sense of the 'Work in Progress'. He is the prose-poet of the half-tone, the neutral tint, the half-formed thought, the hint, the équivoque. When Joyce seeks to present either naked beauty (the "seabird-girl" in the *Portrait*) or unredeemed horror (the "*Walpurgisnacht*" of *Ulysses*) he is, I think, far less happy. The world of Dante was a world of the absolute, whereas Joyce is cognisant of relativity. This accounts for Joyce's aberrations and excesses (for terms themselves are absolutes, and must be rejected by the thorough-going analyst, whether philosophic or aesthetic). But it also saves him from Dante's crudities (the crudities of any hypostasising religion)—such as the attempt to treat states of evil as unvarying mathematic quantities, and apportion to them appropriate degrees of suffering. For Joyce, as for Milton's Satan, "the mind is its own

idealiser as his Protestant townsman Shaw, but unlike him he had—to an extreme degree—the bourgeois sense of family; did he not once condemn Jesus for being a bachelor? As he remained a man of one town, so all his characters would seem to be related—or at least acquainted. He would have been helpless in the presentation of a peasant or a foreigner—even after living in such places as Trieste and Zürich; his conceptions of the aristocracy were (one suspects) those of Gerty MacDowell, and he never seems to have heard of the proletariat. But with all these drawbacks he attains, by his massive symbolism, to a human breadth scarcely equalled by any other novelist. His constant theme is the Biblical one of the son seeking the father and the father the son; it preoccupied him to such a degree that he took a passing interest, I have been told[1]—solely for this reason—in Schiller's dim and fusty Wilhelm Tell. The central episode of *Ulysses* is in fact the one we are not shown— the cuckolding of Leopold Bloom in the sultry afternoon by the jaunty Mr. Blazes Boylan, the sungod-like conqueror in the jingling car. Boylan is, one knows, merely the latest of a series of accepted swains; but the first rift in the Blooms' marital understanding was caused, we are given to understand, by the death of their child Rudy. Since then Bloom for ever seeks, unconsciously, the son who will readjust their relationship and restore his honour. He will never find him, of course; he will

place" and can make a heaven of hell—by the shifting perspectives of the comic. (A grotesque example in *Ulysses*—one of hundreds—is the dog Garryowen of the public-house scene, at one moment a "mangy ravenous brute" that "ate a good part of the breeches off a constabulary man that came round with a blue paper about a license", at another "the famous old Irish red wolfdog setter formerly known by the *sobriquet* of Garryowen", and again figuring in the recollections of Gerty MacDowell as "grandpapa Giltrap's lovely dog Garryowen that almost talked, it was so human".)

[1] My authority is Padraic Colum.

always be, half-contentedly, a cuckold; for man was in fact self-cuckolded when the original Monad fell into multiplicity—by the separation of the Father from the Son through the intermission of Nature, the wife and mother. Such is the sense of Joyce's extremely "family" theology (and incidentally—according to Stephen Dedalus—the meaning of *Hamlet*).

The same theme which is treated farcically in *Ulysses* was a tender, almost elegiac one in that tremendous story *The Dead*. Gabriel Conroy realises that he may never truly possess his wife, for the buried youth Michael Furey can be borne back to her by a chance snatch of song.[1] The true rival to Life, we realise, is Death—whether dead son or dead lover. Joyce, lover of his city, cannot ever possess her; too many shades gather at this "centre of paralysis". Too many lovers have died for Kathleen ni Houlihan—she has given herself to too many strangers. Only by the power of words can Joyce command—in the phrase which falls with the clangour of a bell over so many pages of his work—*the living and the dead*: that dense multifarious life, the swarm of Molly Bloom's gallants, by whom he—the "little man"—is oppressed. For Joyce as for Yeats, the artist is the magician, controlling the spawning images—he is the demiurge breaking the flood; even though the Tower has become the jovial students' Martello Tower, and Kathleen ni Houlihan has shrunk to the Milkwoman.

It seems to me probable that Joyce was influenced, more perhaps than he knew, by the hermeticism of Yeats; in *Stephen Hero* he records the impression made on him, in student days, by the hypnotic and powerful *Rosa*

---

[1] It is ironical to reflect that Joyce's deeply melancholy story *The Dead* is in essence a Christmas ghost-tale, and was probably suggested by Dickens!

Alchemica. The fascination of that work for the Jesuit-bred "apostate" must indeed have been strong. Moreover no youth so proud and ambitious as Joyce was—and who claimed Ireland as his spiritual fief—could have escaped feeling an admiring envy for Ireland's greatest poet; the younger man's admiration for Yeats was indeed always very handsomely acknowledged. He might mock at the "cultic twalette" school;[1] but he was himself, in a sense, a dissident disciple of the Master. That many-sided giant, it may be said, distributed the component elements of his personality among a multitude of followers: F. R. Higgins inherited some part of the lyric richness, Lennox Robinson the dramaturgy, J. M. Hone the Back-to-Berkeley eighteenth-centuryism, Joyce (if I am right) the Cabbalism, the Daedalian artifice, and the romance of the Wandering Jew. It may indeed be doubted whether in Joyce's case the inheritance—though necessary, and in a sense significant—was altogether a benefit; for Joyce's true genius was nearer to that of Shaw and his hero Ibsen—as his Molly Bloom is a more massively-conceived Ann Whitefield. His Celtic-Cabbalist nostalgias gained a (to me) regrettable mastery in the crypto-poeticism of *Finnegans Wake*. Joyce was a poetic realist inoculated by turns with Scholasticism and Esotericism; from the first of these he learned to see himself as St. Stephen the Martyr, from the second as Dedalus the magician. The result is the pedantic allegorism of *Ulysses*—not really necessary to its great symbolic conception, the Swedenborgian correspondences, the

---

[1] Joyce even went so far (when writing *Finnegans Wake*) as to search out the equivalent for "twilight" in Burmese—which happens to be Nyi-ako-mah-thi-ta-this (lit., the time when younger brother meets elder brother, does not recognise him but yet recognises him). It is a good example of Joyce's tendency to wrap up the simple and even sentimental in the esoteric.

almost painful attempt to squeeze the macrocosm into the microcosm—so that the episode associated with the Oesophagus must bring in, with much labour, a *Dr. Salmon*, and that other chapter connected with the Ear must contain the phrase *fit as a fiddle*. The hitching of the stars and worms to Vico's waggon, like the depiction of the organic and inorganic worlds on a notable cathedral-front in Barcelona, was a feat of artifice rather than art—only partially successful in *Ulysses*, a heroic failure in *Finnegans Wake*.

It may be that no nation and no literature can skip any of the "dialectical" phases of its development. The oddity of James Joyce seems to me partly that of a prodigious birth out of time—an oddity favoured certainly, but not engendered, by the artistic climate of the 20th Century. Ireland, owing to her isolation from the European development (and also in part no doubt to foreign domination) had produced no important body of literature during the Middle Age—an age which in her case has continued almost to the present day. Joyce is Ireland's first great native writer—her Dante or her Chaucer; though expressing his age, as every writer should, it was also necessary for him to express, in his manner, those buried ages—to achieve a great collective Yeatsian "dreaming back". He took with immense seriousness his destiny of "forging the uncreated conscience of his race"—so that he had to be, by turns, a St. Augustine crying aloud his sins, a Scholastic glossing on Aquinas, the producer himself of a "Summa" or great synthesis, and finally a Duns Scotus splitting hairs and mangling words. And all the time he was essentially a humorous sceptical Dublin observer—an Everyman among artists, with a schoolboy love of puns, puzzles and indelicacies—sometimes distorted out of nature by these processes, at other times assisted to an immortal symbolisation.

The earlier critics of *Ulysses* thought it a masterpiece— or orgy—of despair and nihilism. Some later critics, in their rather excessive zeal to claim Joyce as a Christian, have declared it a profound and tortured drama of the soul. A few rather stupid critics (like the late A E) have described it as a work of "social surgery". For myself, I confess that I see it primarily as the 18th Century (with less justice surely) saw *Gulliver's Travels*—as "a merry book"; but Joyce is not really a Swift any more than he is a Dante. His characters are not suffering for their sins —they are suffering from "the human situation"; nor are they the expressions of a deeply troubled mind, though—as with so many humorists—they are perhaps antidotes for that condition. They are not all uproari-ously cheerful people of the sort known as "Rabelaisian" —though some of them, like Mulligan and Simon Dedalus, indeed are; but neither are they utterly miser-able people, as in so much modern realism. They are ordinary—not even "charming"—people. Stephen is an irritating prig (for if he is a budding genius this is, rightly, hidden from us),[1] Bloom is a prosy philistine, Mrs. Bloom is a trollop; in a word they are common types. The "happy ending" which lurks round the corner for them is a vulgar *ménage à trois*. They are not made lovable in the Dickens-Dostoievski fashion, nor shown as sensitively evolving in the manner of Proust; their souls have not been chastened by any tragedy nor enriched by any experience—there is not indeed the time for anything to

[1] Except perhaps in the Library-scene. But it was necessary to the scheme of the book that Stephen's theory should be set forth.

happen. And yet, as one closes the book on the last page, one finds—*que voulez-vous?*—that one has grown to like them. One has even the mystical sense—due less to the Homeric parallel than to the range of their wandering meditations—that they are the shadows of a greater *Dramatis Personae.* "Poldy" Bloom seems to be *both* Don Quixote and Sancho Panza; Molly is at once Quixote's Dulcinea and the inn-girl. If they are Yahoos, they are not without their aspirations towards the superior "Houyhnhnm"-state; it is the Time-Flux in which they stick like a birdlime that creates their tragi-comedy. In short I am unable to endorse the lofty pronouncement of Rebecca West:[1] "Nothing is suggested in the course of the book which would reconcile him [Bloom] to the nobility of life. Simply he stands before us, convincing us that man wishes to fall back from humanity into earth, and that in that wish is power, as the façade of Notre-Dame stands above us convincing us that man wishes to rise from humanity into the sky, and that in that wish is power." The squat and spireless Notre-Dame seems in any case ill-chosen for Miss West's fanciful comparison.

It is in this human breadth that Joyce proves himself, most truly, a Catholic—even if he could only exhibit the Catholic temper by rejecting the Catholic faith, as he knew it; for Irish Catholicism, to hold its own in an English-speaking world, has been compelled to take on more than the narrowness of a Protestant sect. The "lapsed" Catholic has in fact peculiar advantages as a comic writer, since he is usually free from the perils of didacticism; and the famous "subtlety" of Jesuitism is near to the comic spirit. It is customary to assert that *Ulysses* is "reeking with the sense of sin"; but here, I

[1] *The Strange Necessity.*

think, it is necessary to make some distinctions. Mr. Bloom, surely, knew little of a "sense of sin"; Mrs. Bloom even less.[1] The "agenbite of inwit" which vexes Stephen Dedalus is filial remorse, and not directly concerned with theological "sin" at all. What the critics really have in mind, I think, is Joyce's deadly clear-sighted, yet almost too-complacent, acceptance of human imperfection; he holds the mirror up to Caliban with a genial grin which is a little too near to being a knowing smirk. We think of Mr. Eliot's "eternal footman" who holds our coat—and snickers; and we are ashamed—for ourselves, and a little also for him. We can enjoy Leopold Bloom, without quite liking to see ourselves in him or him in James Joyce. The impression that Joyce is a sordid writer is due less, I think, to the obscene pages—which in actual fact are few—than to his eerily-objective tone, giving to each fact as it comes precisely the same value as to the next—like a shopman showing his samples—never rising to sociological wrath or hinting at embittered idealism. One has only to compare it with the surgical, almost emetic, brutality of Mr. Aldous Huxley. The modern Anglo-Saxon reader is shocked by an author who sees with such clearness, but shows no desire to

[1] Joyce is both praised and censured for having "reinstated original sin"—which seems odd when one recalls the happy shamelessness of Molly Bloom. Actually Joyce was less interested than almost any writer in moral questions, or in the drama and tension of the will; sin was to him nothing but a jest. Evil for Joyce, is (if anything) metaphysical—not (as with Shaw) ethical and social, nor (as with Swift) a sort of palpable vision of reality. Joyce has a Manichean sense of what Yeats called "the crime of being born"—though he half-negates that sense by the *catharsis* of the comic, so that the terms 'crime' and 'sin' are a little too solemn in this connection. He transfers to the cosmos his natal sentiment of "dear dirty Dublin". Dublin is "the centre of paralysis", but life itself is, almost, a state of paralysis; the Joycean comedy is the comedy of the immobilised act—what Professor E. R. Curtius wittily called *Medicynismus*. Joyce's "love-hate" is nearer to Donne than to Rabelais, Swift or Sterne; but the comparison, it must be admitted, makes Joyce look slightly juvenile.

change or reform, to explain or to excuse—who indulges in no deams of a better future or past—who even in the act of making a commercial traveller Odyssean makes of Odysseus a commercial traveller. Leopold Bloom is the dingiest of heroes—but still a hero; there is the rub. If he were not one we would acclaim James Joyce—the satirist, the idealist, the "savagely serious" critic of society. As it is, we smile a little wryly at the picture, as at the great self-portrait of Rousseau. We are humiliated, and recall uneasily that immortal challenge—

Gather round me the countless host of my fellow-men; let them hear my confessions, lament for my unworthiness, and blush for my imperfections. Then let each of them in turn reveal, with the same frank-ness, the secrets of his heart at the foot of the Throne, and say, if he dare, *I was better than that man.*

Yeats had deplored the coming of the "comic objec-tive spirit", and spoke uncomprehendingly of "that strange man of genius Bernard Shaw"; nevertheless, the Yeatsian play of masks was itself a disciplining of that spirit—its purification from the fearful *opinionatedness* which clogged the Shavian wit. Yeats himself however was far from being free from didacticism; he implied constantly that the Mask was superior to the Face, the "persona" or Platonic Idea to the vulgar reality. We have seen that he attempted to avoid this error by asserting that "Tragedy is gay" and in praising louts and idiots; but a mask, in fact, can never be really gay, and the Yeatsian rogues and strumpets were literary inventions. Joyce—a Shaw without opinions—was nearer than Yeats (in conception at least) to the true artist, with the artist's preference for the "ugly" subject, the artist's turning-away from the merely grand or picturesque. He was a true artist, again, in choosing the only form possible, perhaps, for a literary genius in our "democratic" time—the symbolist novel or prose-epic; for even the stage-drama has to present selected moments and exciting situations. The drama of Shaw and his like did little more than invert the stock-situation. Joyce makes of the ordinary dull moment of consciousness a situation, as the modern physicist calls a fact an "event". Joyce is neither a forward-gazer like Shaw nor a tomb-haunter like Yeats; the world which Yeats longs to escape from and Shaw to set to rights, this cosmic scavenger accepts with an almost canine receptivity for all its sounds and smells. The scrap-heaps and kitchen-middens of his native city—like the slag-pits of the psyche—come to life and dance for him as did the rocks for Orpheus, and the odorific Liffey runs softly till he ends his song; the rounds of a Jewish town-traveller become as timeless as the Old Testament, and a lying-in hospital becomes a symbol of the Inn where symbols are born.

. . . . .

Those persons who find Joyce a harsh and depressing author formed that opinion, one imagines, from reading *A Portrait of the Artist as a Young Man*[1]—a work which for long, owing to the vigilance of customs officials, was a good deal easier to come by than *Ulysses*. The two books are almost opposite in mood; it is as if the author of *The*

---

[1] *A Portrait of the Artist as a Young Man* is somewhat of a misnomer, since the book commences with James Joyce as a baby and is largely a description of his schooldays. The title was doubtless originally intended for the draft-novel now known as *Stephen Hero*, to which it applies with perfect exactness. *Stephen Hero* is of course an immature and ill-written work, and an admirer of Joyce's talent must regret that it should ever have been given to the public.

Magic Mountain (which has some affinities with *Ulysses*)
were to be judged only by *Tonio Kröger*. In the *Portrait*
the only protagonist is the youthful Stephen, who views
himself and his early escapades without irony—indeed
with not a little "ninetyish" romanticism. The interest
of the *Portrait* is that the artist drew it when he was still
very much of a young man, and it is full of the rather
portentous morbidity of adolescence; its emotions are
not remembered—and falsified—in a Goethean tran-
quillity. For in fact our 'teens are always "ninetyish",
and the age of Peter Pan was the age of Dorian Gray.
Joyce had, I believe, escaped from the *selva oscura* by the
time Ulysses was written; he had imagined a healthily
pagan Vergil in Leopold Bloom—an anti-self or "mask"
in the Yeatsian sense—and could describe the lower
regions with the almost tourist-like detachment of a
Dante. Bloom certainly saved James Joyce—if he only
gave rather passing ministrations to Stephen Dedalus.
But in the *Portrait* he is indeed in Hell; and owing to the
peculiar conditions of Catholic Dublin it was a medieval
Hell. James Joyce was one of the few great men of this
century who really in youth encountered religious dogma
—in the old blood-and-thunder sense. It had some
curious results—one of which was that he arrived at
"father-fixation" by way of the theology of Nicaea.

(Thunder is here perhaps the apt word. For Joyce the
thunder, which he always superstitiously feared, possessed
much the same significance as piercing or gleaming light
for Yeats—like that "shout in the street" by which
Stephen defined Deity. It was natural that the theory of
Vico, which traces religion—and consequently society—
to the awesomeness of the thunder, should have made a
ready appeal to him. I need not remind readers of the

importance of thunderclaps in the scheme of *Ulysses* and of *Finnegans Wake*.)

The *Portrait* surprises and fascinates a modern reader by the way it oversteps the centuries between Aquinas and Walter Pater (Pater Noster, as Joyce must surely somewhere have said). Reading it, one would scarcely guess that such events as the Renaissance, the Reformation or the French Revolution had ever occurred. It is a world of "clercs"; the hero, in embracing the profession of an author, is gravely conscious of rejecting one priesthood for another. There 'seem' scarcely to be more possibilities than these two; and the priesthood of letters appears to him, at this time, like some alluring Pagan cult. The description of the young Stephen's transgressions, his repentance, and his brief religious devotionalism, has a reality which moves and shocks us even through the mawkish "aesthetic" prose in which much of it is written. But one fears that these experiences left the man James Joyce—emotionally and intellectually—a little barren and burnt out. The young apostle who set forth in 1902 to smelt his country's conscience was as incurious and closed against life as any of those "wandering scholars" who in such numbers have left her shores. And so, astonishingly, he was to remain through his long and restless existence—as it were a citizen of some Pompeii of the spirit, inwardly petrified by the lava that had fallen on his heart and brain: different indeed from that other wanderer with a religious—though not a medieval—background, D. H. Lawrence. Only his memories—and his comic sense—were left to him; a handful of remembered characters, like a travelling showman's puppets, still accompanied him as he passed to and fro across the ancient agitated continent of Europe—

indifferent to its endless human and cultural variety. He distended them grotesquely—planned their antics with the precision of a ballet-designer—and gave the world that strange, droll, uncomfortable masterpiece *Ulysses*. It was, perhaps, a sufficient achievement for one life—though it presents only one day, and a dull one.

Before he wrote *Ulysses*, however, Joyce produced another work which should be glanced at—the over-ignored play *Exiles*. It is perhaps a not very actable play, though an experienced producer—my friend Charles Turner—is of a contrary opinion. But it should be read by everyone who would understand James Joyce; for it provides an essential link between the lyrical Joyce of *The Dead* and the humorous Joyce of *Ulysses*. The theme is again that of the loneliness of the eternal Husband; in the first story, we saw, he could not possess his spouse because he had a rival in the past, in the second because he has many rivals in the present. Richard Rowan, the Ibsenish hero of *Exiles*, adopts the position of neither interfering nor letting himself be convinced—in one sense or the other. That, it may be said, is the line taken by many honest and sensible married people; but Rowan, for greater self-torment, is in the habit of listening stoically to the confidences of his devoted young wife whom his best friend is courting—though he none the less declares he can never know or fully believe in her. Rowan is an existentialist before Sartre, who imposes on his wife the burden of a wholly gratuitous choice. Is it fanciful to see, in these variations on a theme, illustrations of Joyce's attitude to his country, his religion, and to Life itself? His country has been loved with romantic chivalry in the past—Life is loved grossly, indiscriminately, in every moment of the present—both

repel and abash the jealous artist-lover. There remains
religion; nothing could take the love of God from him
or divide it—but to have it he must believe. And he can
neither believe nor disbelieve. It is a dilemma common
to many sons of the Church, craving for a certainty
which they can never, in the nature of things, attain—
which is indeed the opposite of the human meaning of
"faith". For them, as for the suitors in the Odyssey,
Penelope unweaves by night the sampler she wove by
day; and for Joyce perhaps, in another sense than for
Yeats, the Yeatsian lines are true:

> And he that Attis' image hangs between
> That staring fury and the blind lush leaf
> May know not what he knows, but knows not grief.

Only for Attis substitute Leopold Bloom.

It is merely trite to say that Joyce never really got free
of his religion or his country. We know that, if he had not
become a writer, he had two possibilities open to him:
he could have become a Jesuit Father or (though we hear
less of this in the *Portrait*) a perhaps celebrated concert-
singer—one of those many Dublin tenors who have won
fame in the New World. It seems as if these missed voca-
tions haunted him, ghost-like, to the end—with all the
mystery of that enigma of the *possible* which harried
Stephen Dedalus. (Stephen reflects, meditating on the
personages of history: "Time has branded them and
fettered they are lodged in the room of the infinite possibilities they have ousted. But can those have been possible seeing that they never were?" And in the hospital-
scene he muses theologically on neo-Malthusianism.)
Joyce, after all, was never quite like other writers—born
and not made; his writing was always, in a sense, an

Ersatz—though a magnificent one. He had a philosopher and a poet in him, but the philosopher withered at the touch of the priestly *Doppelgänger*, the poet was dissolved in cloying verse or viscous prose by the spectral impresario. His Jesuit-trained mind remained a little too hard and arid, his middle-class Dublin emotionalism rather too hot and gushing. The mind of Joyce is Stephen Dedalus—clearly an arrested, abnormally static mind; the non-mental part (call it heart, Subconscious or what you will) is represented by the cantatrice Molly Bloom and the various myth-females—whose chief characteristic indeed is not dream or revery but breathless babble. In *Ulysses*—a work which, after all reservations have been made, remains great—Joyce was able to unite the split halves: the Stephen and the Molly of that book, though less complete than the great central creation of "Poldy" Bloom, are at least real and amusing—and they are woven into a truly mighty symbolic frieze. Through the rather unprepossessing mediatorship of Leopold Bloom, Joyce *almost* draws his internal opposites together, but in his other works they soliloquise in the void apart; and it is the spirit of Molly—furbished up to be a Jungian elemental—which rumbles through the rabbit-warren of *Finnegans Wake*. Perhaps one might express Joyce's ultimate failure by saying that Molly in the end absorbs Stephen, Bergsonian gush annihilates Aristotelian form, the Husband-figure no longer stands squarely in the centre and the Ulyssean balance is lost.

· · · · · ·

I never met Joyce, but he is a writer for whom—above all writers perhaps—I feel something akin to affection. He combines—as, apart from him, only some of the great Russians seem able to do—a broad humanity with an unflinching aesthetic detachment. He is greater than the Flaubert of *Bouvard et Pécuchet*, though perhaps not the equal in depth of the Flaubert of the *Tentation*. He has redeemed more sordidness, and won more provinces of reality for art, than, I think, any other writer in English. Even such a grimy story as *Two Gallants*—the first study of a gigolo, as one critic has called it[1]— becomes under his touch a thing of light and air, like some fine Dutch genre-piece. He is, I have already remarked, the one great writer that has come from Catholic Ireland, as Dante was the one great poet of the Middle Age—as though generations had been in labour to produce him. He has celebrated all-oblivious Dublin[2] as Yeats celebrated Maud Gonne, or as Shakespeare celebrated "the Dark Lady"—with the bitterness of an unhappy love; his life is a tale of lonely courage and artistic integrity which shines even through the unsatisfactory biography of Mr. Gorman. I regret therefore that *Finnegans Wake* seems to me to be the "great fall" of Icarus, Humpty Dumpty, or however the genius of Joyce be named. Joyce, it seems to me,—a masterbuilder in the style of his hero Ibsen—, could not ascend a second time to the height of a great epical conception.

James Joyce, as an artist, found himself in a very peculiar and unique position. Speaking a language which—he confessed in the *Portrait*—he felt as alien and refractory, he set himself to describe a life he had known only in childhood and early youth. Imprisoned behind

---

[1] A. J. Leventhal in *The Dublin Magazine*.

[2] To Joyce's curious mind it seemed of extraordinary significance that his leading German disciple and imitator (the author of *Alexanderplatz*) should happen to be named *Doeblin*.

the barriers of his shrinking introversion and failing sight, he lived—in the body at least—in one country, while writing about another, in the speech of a third, an unloved and unknown one. With these impediments—like another Demosthenes—he developed an unheard-of instrumental skill, and exhausted every variation of his single, unpromising-looking, theme; but the theme itself once exhausted, there was nothing left to him but to break the instrument. And this programme accorded well with his Irish iconoclasm and pedantry—the strain in the Irishman for which the best name is "Byzantinism".

Finnegans Wake is, like *Ulysses*, a comic book, but—unlike the other—its humour is for pedants; in it, language itself becomes the Stephen Proto-martyr of Joyce's masochistic wit. Perhaps another way of putting it would be that it is an attempt at a *purely* comic book; it is humour in a void, the smile of a dematerialising Cheshire cat. The puns and coinages, even at their quite fascinating best, suffer from lack of a discernible "point"—they are loose screws which cannot be driven home because the board itself is loose. But too often they verge on that dreariest form of jocosity—the schoolboy howler. (There is, of course, plenty of "point" if you follow the text with a key, an encyclopedia, and a pile of dictionaries.) Beside felicities like "furtivefree years", "der Fall Adams", "the shoutmost shoviality", "muddlecrass", and "the law of the jungerl", we have such melancholy freaks as "Upan-ishadem" (Up Guards and at 'em), "Sea vaast a pool" (Sevastopol), "The Smirching of Venus" and "Ehren gobrawl". There are flashes which have the delicious absurdity of a Marx Brothers film ("The use of the homeborn shillelagh as an aid to calligraphy shows a distinct advance from savagery to barbarism", "never forgetting that both before and after the Battle of the Boyne it was a habit not to sign letters always".) But such humorisms after all do not make *Finnegan* a master-piece, any more than a few grumbling definitions do the same for Johnson's *Dictionary*.

What *Finnegans Wake* is *not* is a profound revelation of the Unconscious, a reflex of the mind in trance—except in the sense in which every work of art is that. Rather, in some ways, it is less one than most, because Joyce is such a very deliberate craftsman. His *monologue intérieur* is very definitely the stream of *consciousness*; and usually, even in *Ulysses*, it is not even any conceivable "stream", but an artful build-up disguised by the omission of "stops". The musings of Mr. Earwicker, in the course of seventeen years' elaboration, must have lost anything they possessed of "the glory and the freshness of a dream". Only—like every humorist—Joyce deliberately makes ordinary life, for his comic purpose, a little more unconscious, automatic and monstrous than it in fact is. Joyce's characters (from the early *Dubliners* onward) are in the plight—familiar in nightmare—of not being able to lift their feet or throw off their "paralysis". But the atmosphere is not one of dread so much as an almost half-witted amusement—the rather gruesome laughter of *John Bull's Other Island*. Like the priest who broke the chalice in his first story, they are discovered "laughing-like softly" to themselves in the confession-box.

Actually there have been many prose-writers whose work has a dream-laden atmosphere; but Joyce is not one of them. Obvious examples are Gogol, Dostoievski, the author of the Apocalypse, Poe, De Quincey, "de Lautréamont", Kafka. It does not appear that Joyce was ever much interested in their work, or in his own dream-states,[1] or (except superficially) in dream-psychology. The authors he admired were rather the vital, *terre à terre*, social and even gregarious authors— Homer, Aristotle, Rabelais (perhaps), Rousseau, Ibsen. Joyce is compared with the Surrealists, but the works of those artists are wholly representational; they show us scenes rendered with photographic verisimilitude, in the midst of which some detail is queerly, horribly, wrong. That Joyce borrowed an incest-motif from Freud and his Four Old Men (probably) from Jung (and perhaps "fur-loined notepaper" from Dali) is less significant than the entirely comic use he makes of this material. Everyone knows that a hint of humour—however fantastic or whimsical—is fatal to a dream-atmosphere; the cracking of the smallest deliberate quip would break the spell. Words—even at their most nonsensical—are intellectual things, and for the dreamer they almost entirely drop away. The more we make our language a pellucid mirror the better it will reflect the turbid happenings of dream; the telescoped phrase cannot reproduce the telescoped image, because it is an effect of human will and contrivance, and rouses the comic sense. The occasional punning ejaculations of sleep or semi-sleep (the product, Freud will have it, of editing by the "Censor") are isolated and discontinuous. Lewis Carroll put his "Jabberwocky" in *Alice in Wonderland*; but the point of that book is that it is a *day*-dream—the deliberate pleasurable invention of a very pedantic don in his lighter moments. *Finnegans Wake* is the most horribly

---

[1] In fact Joyce seems to have dreamt less, almost, than any man alive. It is told of him that he only once had a dream. As might be expected, it was a comic one. He dreamt he was the ace of diamonds, in the act of mounting the stairs!

awake-keeping of all bed-books; it might indeed reflect the writhings and heavings of the insomnia-sufferer. But I can imagine that—suitably illustrated—it might make a capital book for children. The child would fill its fungoid vocables with rich colour that Joyce never imagined; he would wander happily in its mazes, as if in subterranean forests of twisted barley-sugar. I myself in childhood wove unending romances round the absurd names of building-contractors, posted on vacant lots—at that time more numerous and extensive than now.

But indeed if proof be needed that Joyce could not let the Unconscious work for him, it may be found in the manifest failure of the "Circe" episode of *Ulysses*. That chapter, which should be and was intended to be the culminating scene of the book, is probably the least convincing. The description of Joyce as "Rabelais with a nervous breakdown" has some application here (and only here); but of course Joyce never really breaks down, except artistically. "Circe" consists chiefly of clippings from Krafft-Ebbing, the more audacious novelettes, and the Sunday newspapers—all these jumbled together and treated in Joyce's characteristic style of uproarious parody. It is too farcical to give the effect of horror—though it is of course richly "unpleasant"; and Bloom's implied preoccupation with his sexual delinquencies is surely out of character—for Bloom, though a good soul, was not plagued with monkish scruples. No psychology whatever is revealed in this farrago, unless it be the author's own; and it bears little relation to true Surrealist or "dream" writing.[1]

---

[1] The Second Walpurgisnacht (as it might be called) in *Finnegans Wake*—where the protagonists become metamorphosed into characters out of Petronius's Rome —is equally unlike trance or dream, but is much more amusing.

If parallels be sought for *Finnegans Wake* in modernist painting, it seems to me to be the systematisation of the device of the *collage*. The *collage*—the section of newspaper, piece of string or matchbox, carefully wedged like an eye-glass into the corner of a geometric design—may at first have been a justifiable eccentricity: a half-ironic concession to the human hunger for subject-matter, for dressing up the bleak abstraction. But *Finnegans Wake* is a picture so thickly pasted over with every rag, tag and wives' tale of "free association" that the fine Viconian circular design is almost wholly concealed. (And the *collage* also gave to weak artists an excuse for appending their afterthoughts and covering their tracks; *Finnegan* is not only a "riverrun" but a circular electric stair, on which the author's *esprit* is forever trying to catch up with itself.) What the book chiefly reveals, in fact, is the inadequacy of Joyce's culture; it makes no attempt to trace the development of language (as the *Ulysses* hospital-chapter showed, caricaturally, the growth of English prose-style), nor the development of human society. Its history is stage-Irish mythology (Finn McCool, etc.) and memories of the newspaper-reports of the Crimean War; its philology is ephemeral slang, slogans and the equipment of a Cooks' guide. Much of it has gone out of date—and it is hard to think it did not go out of its author's comprehension—during the seventeen years between its commencement and its final printing. Joyce's mind was not furnished like a well-stored museum, but more like a haphazard rag-and-bone shop—not essentially unlike, indeed, the mind of Leopold Bloom. Given a firm design, as in *Ulysses*, he could make the most trivial or sordid material significant, with the mastery of a Rembrandt—so that even the cake

of soap which accompanies the perambulating Mr.
Bloom in his pocket seems to acquire a personality of
its own; but in *Finnegans Wake* the design escaped him.
The result is that this synthesis of all time and all
existence has an extraordinarily musty, fusty flavour;
it is not only Mr. Finnegan's funeral, but—under all
the Einsteinian icing and Freudian frills—the late Queen
Victoria's Diamond Jubilee.

There is, of course, another way of regarding *Finnegans
Wake*, namely as a great prose-poem in celebration of the
river Liffey and the sea—of that element which forms so
much of the beauty of Dublin, and of which the presence
is felt as a persistent *leitmotif* in *Ulysses*. It may be said
that Joyce, though he was somewhat deficient in the red
corpuscles, had Liffey Water in his veins and on his
brain: the river whose name puns so naturally with the
Water of Life. (And how did Joyce fail to play on the
similarity—more than a verbal one—between *aqua pura*
and that fountain of lucent logic, Aquinas?) Many critics
have declared their conversion to *Finnegan* through hearing Joyce's own gramophone-recording of the *Anna Livia*
chapter. But this surely is to judge like the philistines,
who do not *read* poetry, but can occasionally enjoy a
"recitation"—preferably delivered from the bottom of a
hall, by someone with a fine voice. To be very musical
is, it seems, a real hindrance to a writer, for poetic and
musical rhythm are distinct; even Bernard Shaw, we
have noted, though he did not often attempt to write
poetically (when he did, *quel désastre*!), thought that the
beginning and end of poetry was "word-music". Prose-
poetry is usually the refuge of writers who are unsuc-
cessful as poets, and Joyce—though one of the greatest
mere athletes in language there has ever been—was no

true poet; his verses in *Chamber Music* (of which he thought highly, as shown by his continuing the series in *Pomes Penyeach*) are the sort of pieces appropriate to being sung to the piano at drawing-room soirées. The nemesis of the parodist is that he cannot cease from mimicry when he would be most sincere (the jape "sticks", as our elders warned us in the nursery), and Joyce—knowing himself to be a stylist without a style—could only make one by substituting rhythm and onomatopoeia for idea and image.[1] Even in *Ulysses* he often tortured the thoughts of Stephen Dedalus into what reads like bad blank verse. Even the famous vision of the paddling girl in the *Portrait* trembles on the edge of banality. "He was near to the wild heart of life." ". . . girlish, and touched with the wonder of mortal beauty, her face." "A wild angel had appeared to him . . . an envoy from the fair courts of life." Joyce's prose disappointingly flags just where it should soar, for this episode marks a wonderful moment of crisis and liberation. How much more memorable is the (quite incidental) quarrel about Parnell over the Christmas dinner—with its almost comic, yet most moving, close!

Joyce, I say, had considerable verbal music, but much less of verbal magic (though he achieved it more than once—as in the last story of *Dubliners* and the two seashore episodes of *Ulysses*). In this he had as predecessors (though he probably did not know it) the Gaelic "hedge-school" poets of the 18th Century, whose quite empty laments and "visions" are marvels of subtle modulation; a poem by a certain Joseph Lloyd called *Cois Leasa 's me*

---

[1] Joyce carries onomatopoeia to the length of distorting words anagramatically to suggest the munching of food—as for instance, 'kingclud' for 'duckling'. It is a good example of how his method defeats itself; 'duckling' sounds a great deal more like the noise of mastication than 'kingclud'.

go hUaigneach ("Beside the liss and I lonesome") is unsurpassed in sheer virtuosity of vowel-weaving. The Irish,
Wilde said, are too poetical to be poets; and perhaps the
reason is that the Gaelic is too lush and lilting. Joyce
has been called—I forget by whom—a post-Freudian
Swinburne. *Finnegans Wake* is rich in such lines as these—
which have been greatly admired:

> She was just a young thin pale soft shy slim slip of a
> thing then, sauntering by silvamoonlake.

> And low stole o'er the stillness the heart-beats of sleep.

How mellifluous! And how banal! One recalls the
immortal bathos of Alfred Austin:

> The mournful message o'er the waters came,
> "He is not better, he is much the same".

What might not Joyce have been capable of without his
fine sense of humour! Take the following lines, from the
chapter just preceding the dialogue of the washerwomen:

> little oldfashioned mummy, little wonderful mummy,
> ducking under bridges, bellhopping the weirs, dodg-
> ing by a bit of bog, rapid-shooting round the bends,
> by Tallaght's green hills and the pools of the phooka
> and a place they call it Blessington and slipping sly by
> Sallynoggin, as happy as the day is wet, babbling,
> bubbling, chattering to herself, deloothering the fields
> on their elbows leaning with the sloothering side of her,
> giddy-gaddy, grannyma, gossipaceous Anna Livia.

The patter is pretty enough—it is in fact almost impossible to describe the progress of a river without writing

a sort of poetry; but why does it bring to my mind certain lines we all learned at school, and which no one, certainly, ever claimed to be great literature?—

> Should you ask me, whence those stories, whence those legends and traditions, with the odours of the forest, with the dew and damp of meadows, with the curling smoke of wigwams, with the rushing of great rivers, with their frequent repetitions, and their wild reverberations, as of thunder in the mountains. . . .

(Especially the repetitions and reverberations.) The evocation of Anna Livia takes its place, in the end, only a little above Minnehaha, Laughing Water. (Minnehaha—obviously a pun in three languages: French *minet*, German *Minne*, Persian *Mene*. *Haha*—a hearty laugh—is clear enough, though the sound of strangulation may also be intended, and perhaps water running out of a bath-tub: not to forget the Old French *haha*, "an obstacle interrupting one's way sharply and disagreeably". The whole may be read from left to right or from right to left, or you may start in the middle. Minnehaha is not only the Indian myth-heroine, but a forgotten music-hall celebrity, Minny Harper. And so on. It will be seen that the scholars of the New World have enough of this sort of research to occupy them till Tibb's Eve.)

The ambition to write a "Prophetic Book" has ruined more than one artist. Joyce regretted that Yeats did not use the theories of *A Vision* for a work of art on the grand scale; but Yeats's "Instructors"—or his aesthetic instinct —wisely forbade such an attempt. He had the unfortunate example of his first teacher, Blake, for a deterrent.

Joyce, unlike Yeats and Blake, was neither poet nor philosopher—though he was a genuinely philosophical novelist and an intensely poetic short-story writer. There was, however, a restless Irish *ambitieux* in him, forever pressing towards new conquests—a daemon such as inhabited no other writer I can think of but Rousseau. The youthful Stephen Dedalus had declared that he felt himself to be the slave of two masters—the imperial British state and the holy Roman catholic and apostolic church. From the first he received—with an inner resistance—his language, from the second his philosophy; and though he was to show in *Ulysses* that he could prose it with Malory or Macaulay, and in the *Portrait* that he could discuss aesthetics with Aquinas, this was all in the nature of a very Irish bravura-performance. It is true that in the process he had created an unforgettable gallery of character-studies—characters which indeed attain to the status of symbols or archetypes—and had written one of the great comic books of the world, worthy to rank with Gargantua, Gulliver or Tristram Shandy; but with these achievements he was by no means content. He had still to fulfil that rather bombastic programme of his youth—to forge in the smithy of his soul the uncreated conscience of his race. But how was he, self-outcast and—with all his miscellaneous erudition—oddly ignorant of his time, to do any such thing? True, he carried Ireland everywhere with him like a pilgrim's pack, but his Ireland was the Dublin of the Pigott Forgeries, "Erin go Bragh", and the joke-giant Finn McCool. Of the Irish language, and the forces that were shaping the Ireland of today, he knew nothing—had never, in his impatient youth, wished to know anything. *Tant pis!* He would bring together these miserable shreds of Hiberniana and the little he knew of post-Scholastic European thought—he would do it by a daring exploitation of those new theories of the "Collective Subconscious" which, it so happened, were stirring in Zürich during the time of his residence there. He would imagine a great dream in which the Vico Road at Dalkey merged with Giambattista Vico's cycles, in which the notable bookshop of Messrs. Browne and Nolan was one with Giordano Bruno of Nola, in which the Phoenix Park (a traditional mis-spelling, incidentally, of the Gaelic name) became the *locus* of Adam's Fall (that "*felix* culpa") and the Phoenix's fiery rebirth. He would invent a new language to fit this material, as the exiled Dante created, in effect, a new language (not, it is true, a nonsense-language) to write the Divine Comedy. The experiment was arresting, and—up to a point—amusing; but it was not very like a dream. He took seventeen years over it, and the result was the weirdest "folly" in the history of verbal architecture. As one of Joyce's earnest apologists[1] has phrased it, "It remains a brilliant and formidable feat of literary pioneering, to which all future artists in words must be in debt, *if only because it shows some things to be impossible.*" (Italics mine.) I think one really cannot say any fairer than that!

Nevertheless *Finnegans Wake* is in a sense an important book; and one feels with a certain exasperation that—only for Joyce's stage-Irishry, his pedantry, and his megalomania—it might have been a great book. It is the one true nature-myth of modern writing which springs straight from the urban scene, without the interposition of literature or folklore. Its conception of the two

[1] L. A. G. Strong, *The Sacred River.*

washerwomen, washing their dirty linen—in all senses—
on the twin river-banks, till with gathering night they
are metamorphosed to tree and stone—a Tree of Life
and a Stone of Destiny—, this is worthy of the imaginative genius who wrote *The Dead*; and it moves us the
more by the fact that, at the time, the twilight was
gathering over Europe, and the wireless was twittering
excitedly through the gloom (without, unfortunately, a
corresponding lapse into silence). One is reminded of the
Irish epic, the Cattle-Raid of Cuailgne—similarly grand,
simple and austere in plan, similarly extravagant, over-
worked and unequal in its detail—the material of a great
work of art which somehow never got composed: the
hero who holds a ford against gathering invading hosts,
while his countrymen are smitten by an offended goddess with that peculiar condition (so often referred to in
Joyce's writings) of "paralysis". In that epic there is also
a washer of clothes—the traditional Washer at the Ford
who portends the death or transmigration of the hero;
and one is struck by the atavism which made these pre-
Christian patterns recur in a cosmopolitan author's
20th-Century extravaganza.

"All the rivers run into the sea, yet the sea is not full:
unto the place from whence the rivers come, thither they
return again." There is nothing new under heaven;
Mother-Complex and Death-Wish are as old as the Book
of Ecclesiastes. Joyce, to whom life was exile and exile
was life, had a single theme beneath all his buffooneries
—the return of Odysseus-Bloom to his home, the return
of the raindrop to the ocean.[1] He is that typically

---

[1] The last paragraph of *Finnegans Wake*—full of the premonition of death—has,
I think, a much greater effectiveness than any other part of the book. Here the
polyglot language ceases to be a humorism, and becomes truly suggestive, like the
mysterious nonsense-ending of an old song or tale.

modern phenomenon, the "displaced person"—forever seeking, as in the Aristotelian physics and cosmology, "his own place". *Ulysses* has been called, with some reason, a book of wombs and tombs. It takes human existence on a dull day of a dull year in a dull town, places it like a drop of water on a slide under a microscope, and reveals its very substance and texture—its swarming denizens grotesquely magnified. "Finnegan's Wake"—title of a song in the worst music-hall "broth of a bhoy" manner—is redeemed by the unexpected richness of its overtones: the antediluvians come again, their "wake" (death-watch) is also an awakening. "Harry me, marry me, bury me, bind me" is the nostalgic refrain of the book so-named—actually a Joyceanisation of Vico's spiral, but tantalising one like some fortune-teller's rigmarole as old as the Pyramids. It is related that Joyce once remarked—explaining why he did not write stories of love and crime—that life and death were of quite sufficient interest to him; and indeed he was far too conscious of life as a dream to be specially interested—as Yeats for instance was—in dreaming. He was forever pinching himself, with the pincers of his irony, to awaken from "the nightmare of history"—the fearful load of the Everyday. His obsession with death makes him seem more important to us—nearer to our modern desolation —than Yeats or Shaw, the spiritualist and the evolutionist. He was no bustling striving public figure, but an exile, a bohemian, the very "Prodigal Son"; and he knew the meaning of the New Testament phrase "to go to the Father".

And yet there is something in Joyce, when all is said, that one does not find wholly delightful; something over-sly, jeering and triumphing, as of the dissipated

seminarist[1]—something a little unclean even in his mania
for tearing words to pieces, like a mischievous child picking
the wings off flies. Words for him, one feels, were husks,
from which the vital content had perished—fit to be
played with at thimble-and-pea games. With his perverse pride he was resolved that language should owe
everything to him—that there should be no reciprocal
obligation. "I can do everything with language", he
boasted—a vaunt more worthy of a juggler or flea-trainer
than of a creative genius. With an almost senile glee he
puns his chosen nickname Shem with Sham, and hints
that his forged metal is "forged" coin. His interest in
Cabbalism—like that of some French *symbolistes*—was in
part, one suspects, a search for the grammar of power;
for Joyce was near enough to supernatural religion to
feel, superstitiously, that words are talismans, and that
the Church, in her formularies, possesses a real magic
well. (And it should be remembered that the notion of
a secret language—known to "adepts", and destined
to supersede all existing languages—was at all times
a Cabbalistic doctrine.) I have suggested that Joyce's
arcana were a legacy from Yeats; but Yeats's attraction
to the "secret tradition" was largely a search for mystery
and colour—it was the Protestant artist's nostalgia for
hierarchic speech and ritual. But in Joyce's world there
is little mystery and no colour—everything is as grey
and stale as "blasphematory spits" or "quashed quota-
toes". Joyce could command words and make them
serve him, but—similarly to Shaw with his horrible pro-
posals for phonetic spelling—he did not love them. The
proof is that this most individualistic of all writers has,

[1] It should be understood that I am speaking here only of Joyce in his writings.
The man himself seems to have been altogether sweet and gracious.

like Picasso, no individual style. He is as it were an impersonal machine in which words are crushed and pulped. He is a great pattern-maker, but his patterns seem superimposed on the brute-reality as though by an industrial process. If Shaw was the first journalist Joyce was, essentially, the first scenario-writer.

And similarly Joyce's attitude to the world is not quite that of an enjoyer. Molly Bloom may say Yes to existence (with perhaps an incongruous reminiscence of *Sartor Resartus*), but Joyce does not—quite; and consequently we do not altogether delight in Molly, as we do for instance in Somerset Maugham's Rosie of *Cakes and Ale*. Joyceans may see her as a sort of Pagan fertility-goddess; but of course—to be perfectly accurate—she is done with child-bearing, and her Yes is of a different kind. (And Homer's Penelope, by the way, is chiefly remembered for saying No.) "Poldy" Bloom goes home to sleep in conjugal sheets that still bear the impress of Blazes Boylan—and though this is possibly better than the bloody conclusion of the Odyssey, we cannot help feeling that we, as well as Bloom, are a little soiled. Bloom may represent Eternity and Boylan may signify Time—its active and usurping Shadow; but though one may be —I certainly am—tickled into hilarity by such a fancy, one is scarcely moved to elation. It may be said that in all mythologies (and Joyce is best considered as a modern mythologist) there is much that is repulsive or trivial; and that there is plenty of the humour of soiled bed-linen in such classic farce as *The Merry Wives of Windsor*. That is quite true, but there is also freshness of language and visual imagery, and it is the comparative lack of these in the world of *Ulysses* which makes that world, in the end, oppressive. It is Rabelais without the Renaissance sense of a new dawn, for Joyce—a bourgeois of the bourgeois—knows nothing of the 20th Century;[1] such a writer as D. H. Lawrence, in spite of his extravagances, was much nearer to the primitive and self-renewing energies of the Time-Spirit. I do not of course suggest that Joyce is a pornographic writer—he was undoubtedly sincere in his bracketing of pornography with didacticism as impure art; and in fact one does not get the feeling I speak of from the realistic sketches in *Dubliners*. It is in fact the comedy-contrast between the cosmic allegory of *Ulysses* and *Finnegan* and their abundantly nauseous detail that leaves us, in spite of all the zestful virtuosity, with a certain feeling of distaste. It is the borderline between symbolism and caricature, and Joyce—a displaced person with dubious passports—will not let himself be caught straying outside that No-Man's-Land. His work is the Music of the Spheres—and it is "Chamber Music": as he might put it, the macrocosm and the *micturocosm*. *Ulysses* has, in a sense, the mystical inclusiveness of the Hebrew canticle,

> All ye beasts and cattle, praise ye the Lord!
> Praise him and magnify him for ever.

Yet, if you sing (as a modern mystic ought perhaps to be able to do),

All ye cancer-germs and spirochaetes, praise ye the Lord, etc.

---

[1] If anything could make me uneasy in my admiration of Joyce, it would be to see him described—by a writer in *transition*—as "the Central Luminary of Modern Literature, around which revolve the Fiery Comets of the True Dawn". (Capitals *not* mine.) Joyce himself, on the other hand, had his moments of self-doubt, which prove—to me—his utter and painful sincerity. Speaking of his 'Work in Progress' (as it was then called) he said "Perhaps it is craziness. One will be able to judge in a century." (Quoted by Louis Gillet in *transition* 1932.)

the effect (I think it will be agreed) is just a little dubious and equivocal. A slightly loutish Blake, Joyce sees Infinity in a long nose[1] and Eternity in a belch. He can be—and has been—hailed both as a great Christian and a great anti-Christian writer;[2] his mind has more obliquities and ambiguities (though used for an artistic purpose) than St. Alphonsus Liguori knew of. The pun—it seems unnecessary to point out—is a two-faced thing, and its other name is the *double entente*; puns have been used as hoops to hold truths together, but Joyce uses the

[1] I am not here indulging in a mere phrase. The Second Book of *Finnegans Wake* concludes with a table of numerals, rendered in what Joyce perhaps imagined to be Gaelic, and equated with various strange abstract concepts (puns, but not happy ones)—such as "pantocracy", "bimutualism", etc. But *cush* (five—which is not however Gaelic) refers us to the footnote "Kish is for anticheirst, and the free of my hand to him!" The footnote is embellished with a rudely-drawn *fico*. According-ing to Messrs. Campbell and Robinson's *Key* we are to see here the decad of the Cabbalistic Sephiroth, representing the descent of Spirit into Matter. Half-way down the ladder, the number of God (3) and that of Nature (4) become the sign of Man (5). With these, not unprofound, ideas I am familiar as a philosopher; but they are hardly very worthily represented by the Nose (symbolising Divine Afflatus) and the five outspread Fingers of the (in every sense) rude drawing! If this symbolism has any meaning, it means that the Temporal is a highly regret-table Gesture of the Eternal, born of some discreditable impulse of self-extension: a Manichean doctrine which accords in fact with the spirit of Joyce's writings, and, in general, with the Irish religious temper.

[2] See for instance the review of *Ulysses* in *The Dublin Review* (Summer number 1922): "Without grave reason or indeed the knowledge of the Ordinary, no Catholic publicist can even afford to be possessed of a copy of this book, for in its reading lies not only the description but the commission of sin against the Holy Ghost. Having tasted and rejected the devilish drench, we most earnestly hope that this book be not only placed on the Index Expurgatorius, but that its reading and communication be made a reserved case. . . . Doubtless this book was intended to make angels weep and to amuse fiends, but we are not sure that those embattled angels of the Church, Michael's host, will not laugh aloud to see the failure of this frustrated Titan as he revolves and splutters hopelessly under the flood of his own vomit." This fulmination may be contrasted with the pronounce-ment of T. S. Eliot that Joyce is the most orthodox of writers, with the *Osservatore Romano's* praise of his work, and with the statement of Thomas Merton (author of *Elected Silence*) that Joyce's writings contributed to his conversion. (The reason which Mr. Merton gives, however, is peculiar and not reassuring. The crude Hell-sermon in the *Portrait* delighted him, it seems, on account of its "efficiency, solidity and drive". Mr. Merton was impressed by its "expertness"; he was "edified". The age we live in has rediscovered the uses of terrorism; but Joyce, so far as one can gather, had his faith killed by such preaching.)

pun rather as a wedge to drive them apart. Joyce is both *voyant* and *voyeur*, delighting in such conceits as "Entwine our arts with laughters low" and "Let us pry". He is like Averroes and Maimonides in Stephen Dedalus's vision (scarcely a very accurate one) of those philosophers: "dark men in mien and movement, flashing in their mocking mirrors the obscure soul of the world, a darkness shining in brightness which brightness could not comprehend" (an echo here, perhaps, of the famous Gaelic vision-poem, *Brightness of Brightness*—as well as of the Gospel of St. John).

.   .   .   .   .

Upon such an artist as Joyce no simple judgment is possible. From one viewpoint he is more insidiously destructive than any writer of our anarchic time; he demolishes, not beliefs and venerated customs, but the very conditions of thinking. He uses the Word to break down the Thing and the Thing to ridicule the Word— the complete and utter metaphysical dualist, or comic Manichean. The metaphysics of the student, the science of the practical man, alike end "where all the ladders start"—in the fleshly ruminations of the Eternal Feminine. Yeats, in his later verse, had overpraised mere spawning life; with Joyce, the words themselves spawn. And yet, to a certain extent, he discovers new energies in language and new values in dross and dullness—like a chemist producing silks out of pulp; with him we feel ourselves always in Olympus, even if it is a grotesque Olympus. By his splitting of every hair that divides false and true, fair and foul, he would seem to have burst that cerebral atom, the *concept*—the very rock on which any mental order must be built. Like his fellow-exile of

Zürich days—Nicolai Lenin—he has started an avalanche that cannot easily be measured. And yet, when the explosion has subsided, all that we see is Mr. Bloom—very much larger than life—continuing on his rounds, Anna Liffey slip-slopping between her banks: perhaps nothing but empty solemnity has been destroyed—perhaps the irony was more human than we thought it. He knew, I think, not much more about the Unconscious than the petty nobleman Lenin knew about the Proletariat, or than the romantic adventurer Rousseau knew about the "Canaille"; nevertheless he, more than any man, has unleashed that psychical rabblement. After him, like the hen Belinda in *Finnegans Wake* (brought in apparently—with enormous ingenuity—solely for the sake of this word-play) we "start from scratch". What an irony that the century which has rediscovered Aquinas should have also called forth—like a derisive echo—this jesting, word-mincing Scholastic! And yet he is in a sense the last great Christian, and calls us to a fabulous, a farcical—but not really a corrupt or Satanic—communion. His own profane jingle happens to describe him exactly—himself is the tout that pumped the stout in the tavern that Jack built.

Such figures as James Joyce exceed the day-to-day plan, the merely rational schedule; and the total plan is hidden from us. Mental order, like social, ends always by becoming oppressive, lop-sided, by galling the human pack-animal at some point—whereupon it has, more or less violently, to be thrown off. It is sweet and decorous to laugh, occasionally, even before the suburban altars of Hymen and Cloacina. One can only say, "This writer eases certain frictions for me, resolves certain tensions". Personally I may avow that *Ulysses* eases large spaces of my life—*Finnegans Wake*, at present, comparatively minute ones. But I know that, some day or other, I may turn to Joyce's second and darker decoction with a real refreshment. I may look at these words I now use—the words (I hope) of "the Queen's English", which at present suit me well enough—and see them as awkward opaque things, deforming more than they express of my individual "truth". Then I may throw them willingly, like shaped stones, into that rushing gurgling river of Joysick Esperanto, to be worn round and clean by its waves of sound and association. Until then I must remain, with regard to Joyce's total achievement, "in twosome twiminds"—a state of indecision harmonising with that Dusk which broods, like a soul waiting to be born, over so many pages of his prose.

. . . . .

In mid-January 1941, war was general over Europe; and the deciphering of the meaning of *Finnegans Wake* (printed shortly before the Outbreak) was the least of the headaches of the old continent. In England, the rather less sibylline utterances of another Mr. Joyce were, just then, engaging widespread amused attention. British preparations were proceeding for the next stage of the successful Desert offensive—the capture of the beleaguered port and naval base of Tobruk. Greek troops were reported to have entered the key-city of the Albanian front, and the Italians were retreating in disorder into the mountains. The British Fleet Air Arm had again attacked the Sicilian bases. London had experienced another fire-*blitz*, but the attack was defeated by the keenness and energy of the fire-fighters; a small messenger-boy was seen calmly smothering a fire bomb with his tin helmet. In Washington, deliberations on the Lease-and-Lend Bill had opened in an atmosphere of optimism, and the feeling that the aid envisaged by the measure was all that was necessary to carry the Axis further down [the road of defeat. It was anticipated (correctly, as the event proved) that some sort of offensive move on the part of Germany was to be expected in the near future. . . . But we may be certain that James Joyce in his hospital at Zürich—even if he were still able to think of anything—was thinking of none of these things. During the months which preceded the Fall of France—and his enforced withdrawal to this city of old association—he had paid little attention to the march of events; his radio-set would be constantly tuned in on remote neutral Dublin, and on no other station. The Finnish War, it is true, through the coincidence of nomenclature—the giant Finn and the "Russian general" of Crimean memory in *Finnegans Wake*—had aroused in him a momentary excitement; but that was all. Now as the shades thickened over the old Europe— the Europe which, even in its ruin, still loved leisure, learning and puns—so they were thickening around the modern Rabelais. A greater, a more gracious time had gone. Earwicker, Stephen Dedalus—Bloom himself— had begun to look old-fashioned and rather pitiful, like a music-hall deserted; but of this their creator was happily unaware. He was carried back, one may fancy, to a late Autumn in Dublin thirty-seven years previously, when he and his young spouse Nora Barnacle were sleeping beside their sparse luggage in the Grosvenor Hotel, before setting out early on the morrow to far-away old-world Trieste. He was listening, perhaps, to a sound unusual and always rather arresting in his country, and which—to his preternaturally sensitive hearing—carried a rumour of the distant, the ultimate things. In the closing words of his greatest story—which, only for one slightly over-precious verb, would rank among the most magical passages in English prose—"his soul swooned slowly as he heard the snow falling faintly through the universe and faintly falling, like the descent of their last end, upon all the living and the dead."